ISBN 978-0-260-55202-0
PIBN 10955735

MASSACHUSETTS
STATE TEACHERS COLLEGE

BRIDGEWATER

ESTABLISHED : : : 1840

CATALOG FOR 1937-1938

COMMONWEALTH OF MASSACHUSETTS

DEPARTMENT OF EDUCATION

THE COMMONWEALTH OF MASSACHUSETTS

DEPARTMENT OF EDUCATION

JAMES G. REARDON, Commissioner of Education

Division of Elementary and Secondary Education and State Teachers Colleges

PATRICK J. SULLIVAN, Director

FLORENCE I. GAY, Supervisor of Elementary Education

ALFRED R. MACK, Supervisor of Secondary Education

RAYMOND A. FITZGERALD, Supervisor of Educational Research and Statistics and Interpreter of School Law

THOMAS A. PHELAN, Supervisor in Education of Teacher Placement

RAYMOND H. GRAYSON, Supervisor of Physical Education

CALENDAR
1937–38

FIRST SEMESTER

September 13 . . . . Training School Opens

September 13–14 . . . . Second Entrance Examinations

September 20 . . . . Teachers College Opens

October 12 . . . . Columbus Day

November 11 . . . . Armistice Day

November 24, noon, to November 29 . . . . Thanksgiving Recess

December 18 to January 3 . . . . Christmas Recess

January 28 . . . . Close of First Semester

SECOND SEMESTER

January 31 . . . . Beginning of Second Semester

February 19–28 · . . . . Winter Recess

April 15 . . . . Good Friday

April 16–25 . . . . Spring Recess

May 30 . . . . Memorial Day

June 2–3 . . . . First Entrance Examinations

June 5–10 . . . . Commencement Week

Sessions

Sessions are from 8.40 o'clock A.M. to 12.30 o'clock P.M., and from 1.30 o'clock P.M. to 3.15 o'clock P.M. There are no sessions on Saturday.

Telephones

The college may be reached by telephone through the following numbers of the Bridgewater Dial Exchange:

Office of President	422
Business Office	422
Office of Dean of Women, Boyden Hall	664
Training School	410
Gymnasium	661
Office of Dietitian	972
Power Plant	2421
Tillinghast Hall (pay station)	833
Woodward Hall (pay station)	802

TABLE OF CONTENTS

HISTORY

Since colonial days, Massachusetts has taken seriously the business of educating its children. Under the early conditions, when the three R's were sufficient in the schoolroom, it was thought that almost any literate person was qualified to teach. In later days, however, far-sighted people began to see that the growing demands upon the schools made it impossible longer to depend upon untrained teachers. The story of Horace Mann is familiar to all in Massachusetts. He, more than any other one individual, was responsible for the ideal of "a trained teacher for every child." With the help of many who joined with him, he succeeded in persuading the General Court to try the experiment of starting Normal Schools for the training of teachers.

Of the three schools thus opened, Bridgewater was one, and it has continued ever since, with no loss of time, in the place where it began its work. Normal School and Teachers College, Bridgewater has had an uninterrupted tradition. Throughout its nearly one hundred years of service to the children and youth of the Commonwealth, Bridgewater ideals, "the Bridgewater spirit," have had a very real existence and influence in the field of education.

The school has had only six principals and presidents during its long history. The first principal, Nicholas Tillinghast (1840–1853), "by sheer skill and genius" made the school a success. He had no easy task. Normal Schools were definitely on probation. Many people thought the whole idea ill-advised and even un-American. The school itself was dreadfully hampered by lack of financial support. On September 9, 1840, its doors were opened, in the old Town House, with 28 students. The total expenditure of money up to this time was $1250. Six years later the first Normal School building in America was built on the present grounds of the College. Mr. Tillinghast worked with untiring industry and fiery zeal to make the Normal School worthy of its high privilege. He made his school neither narrowly academic nor narrowly pedagogical. Rather, he was committed to the definite professional aim of sending out educated men and women who were interested in skillful teaching as a fine art. In spite of the limitations of the school, in spite of opposition from without, "an unusual number of educational leaders were inspired and developed" who, zealous young pioneers that they were, profoundly influenced the schools of Massachusetts and of many other states.

Marshall Conant, friend of Mr. Tillinghast, became the next principal. During the seven years of his service (1853–1860), in a time of depression, both financial and educational, he found scope for his remarkable personal talents of enthusiasm and genial leadership. He was a scientist; and while he enlarged the scientific studies and equipment of the school, he also started the movement toward a systematic pedagogy which was to be carried on by his successor.

With the entrance of Mr. Albert G. Boyden upon his long period of service (1860–1906) the school became thoroughly established. Mr. Boyden had served as assistant to both of the preceding principals. He carried forward their ideals while making his own contribution to the growth of Bridgewater. Mr. Boyden was interested primarily in psychology, and its effect upon teaching. He was also an administrative genius, in the days when each principal of a State Normal School set and supervised the policy of his own school. As time went on he gathered about him a faculty selected primarily for their conscientious scholarship, and devotion to education. He integrated the school by his own strong, clear-cut personality, which dominated every department. The school grew steadily in space, equipment, and number of students. It changed to keep pace with the advances of educational thinking, adding kindergarten, gymnasium, new departments, and new ideas, but always centering about psychology, philosophy, and pedagogy, and always keeping the "Bridgewater spirit."

In 1906, when Mr. Albert Boyden retired, his son, Arthur Clarke Boyden, became principal. The principalship of Dr. A. C. Boyden saw many changes. The number of students increased rapidly. Education was beginning to be studied as a science. Psychology, and consequently pedagogy, were being resurveyed, with results at first chaotic, but afterwards stimulating. Dr. Boyden was himself a keen student of men and affairs, and an inspired interpreter and teacher of history. A teacher himself, he chose his faculty for their teaching ability. The four-year course which had temporarily lapsed, was again introduced, and gradually dominated the school until the shorter courses almost disappeared, even before they were formally discontinued by the Department of Education.

In the latter part of 1924 the school building and two of the dormitories burned. However, with the loss of only a few days, the school activities continued under make-shift conditions until the new building was opened in 1926. In 1932, by act of the General Court, Bridgewater, together with the other State Normal Schools, became a State Teachers College, of which Dr. Boyden became the first president. The change, which brought the teacher training institutions of Massachusetts into line with other similar institutions, gave them the needed prestige, and the privilege of granting the degree now considered essential to graduates.

At the death of Dr. Boyden, in 1933, Dr. Zenos Edmund Scott was installed as second president of the College. The present trend of the College is toward a broadened and deepened scholarship, always as a preparation for better teaching service. At the resignation of Dr. Scott in 1937, Mr. John J. Kelly, long Dean of Men in the College, was appointed president.

The number of students admitted to the school is limited by the Department of Education. Conditions of admission can be found elsewhere in this catalogue; they are designed to select, as far as possible, students who sincerely desire to live up to the College motto, "Not to be ministered unto, but to minister," and to prepare to serve the community to the best of their ability. The following quotation from the Bridgewater catalogue of 1844 still remains true:

"This institution . . . claims . . . to afford aid and encouragement to those faithfully striving to learn their duty. Such, only, are wanted at this School. It should be distinctly understood that this School has no power to make good teachers of the dull or the idle. . . . A teacher must educate himself. This institution will assist him."

The "Bridgewater spirit" has been a reality for nearly a hundred years. It is a great heritage to carry into the next century.

The State Teachers College at Bridgewater is modern in buildings and equipment. Its campus is occupied by Boyden Hall, built in 1926, which contains classrooms, library, laboratories, lockers and rest rooms for commuting students, the Horace Mann Auditorium, and administration offices; Tillinghast Hall, with dining-room, large and small reception rooms, kitchens, and girls' dormitory rooms; Woodward Hall, the largest of the dormitories, which also has reception rooms, kitchenette, and recreation rooms; the Training School, an elementary school under joint town and state control, where junior students spend their first period of practice teaching under critic teachers; Gates House, and the college heating and lighting plant. Playing fields, a large garden and a greenhouse add to the usefulness and attractiveness of the college grounds.

Bridgewater is so near Boston that students share many of the cultural advantages of that city. Every year large groups visit the Flower Show, The Arboretum, the museums, operas, theaters, and symphony concerts; while smaller groups make various excursions to other points of interest, in many places.

STUDENT ACTIVITIES

General Statement.—A varied program of activities is carried on at the college with a four-fold purpose: recreation, social enjoyment, cultural opportunity, and training in leadership. So many clubs and groups are meeting that every student should be able to find one where he may get pleasure and profit. Besides, he will find his experience valuable when he is expected to take responsibility, as a teacher, in the club program of his school.

The Student Co-operative Association

The Student Co-operative Association shares the responsibility for carrying out the policies of the college; initiates movements for the betterment of student welfare; supervises certain phases of the student social life of the college; and in many ways materially adds to the happiness and success of college life.

All students are members of this Association. Most of the offices are elective. Since students are chosen because of their ability, scholarship, co-operation, and leadership, membership upon the boards and councils of the Association is considered an honor.

Athletic Associations

The Women's Athletic Association fosters recreational activities, including games, dancing, outing activities, sports, and so forth.

The Men's Athletic Association, in addition to its campus activities, carries on a program of team-games and sports in soccer, basketball, baseball, and tennis.

Membership in the Associations is automatic with membership in the college; participation in the various activities is optional.

Campus Comment

The college monthly, and "Alpha", the annual, record the activities of college life.

Each publication is managed by a board of editors whose membership is chosen by examination, recommendation, or popular election.

Men's Club

This group has both social and professional aspects. During each year it hears speakers on various topics, and initiates movements of interest to the men of the college.

Dramatic Club, Glee Clubs, and Orchestra

These organizations are open to both men and women. They give excellent public performances, and also contribute much to different phases of college life. In addition, smaller and less formal musical groups provide an even greater range of opportunity.

Camera Club, Garden Club, and Hobby Club

Opportunities are provided for recreation and for profitable pursuit of outside interests.

French Club, German Club, Science Club, Topics of the Day Club, Kindergarten-Primary Club, and Library Club

These clubs welcome those who have special abilities or interests in their several fields, and offer social contacts as well.

FACULTY

The Teachers College

John J. Kelly . . . . President
Fitchburg; B.S. in Ed., Boston University; Boston College

Charles E. Doner . . . . Supervisor of Penmanship
Zanerian College; Denison University

Brenelle Hunt . . . . Psychology
Bridgewater; Harvard; Columbia

Frieda Rand . . . . Music; Supervision in Training School; Glee Club; Orchestra
B.A., Mount Holyoke; New England Conservatory of Music; Columbia

Louis C. Stearns . . . . Elementary School Science; Greenhouse; School Gardens
Bussey Institute, Harvard

S. Elizabeth Pope, Dean of Women . . . . Introduction to Education
Framingham; B.S., M.A., Columbia

Edith H. Bradford . . . . French; German
B.A., Tufts; M.A., Middlebury; Paris

Priscilla M. Nye . . . . Supervisor of Art
Massachusetts School of Art; International School of Art

M. Katharine Hill . . . . Literature
B.L.I., Emerson; Harvard; Columbia

Joseph I. Arnold . . . . Sociology; Economics
B.A., Centre; M.A., Columbia; Ph.D., Harvard

Julia C. Carter . . . . Library
B.A., Middlebury; New York State Library School; Bread Loaf School of English

Ruth E. Davis . . . . English
Bridgewater; B.S., M.A., Boston University

Olive H. Lovett . . . . English
B.A., University of Montana; Ed.M., Harvard

Lois L. Decker . . . . Physical Education; Supervision in Training School
B.A., University of Wisconsin; M.A., New York University

George H. Durgin . . . . Mathematics
B.A., Ed.M., Harvard

Alice B. Beal . . . . Director of Training
Bridgewater; B.S., New York University; Ed.M., Boston University

Cora M. Vining . . . . Library Assistant
B.S. in Ed., Bridgewater; Simmons; Boston University

Paul Huffington . . . . Geology; Geography
B.E., Normal University; A.M., Clark; University of Chicago

Mary V. Smith . . . . History
Worcester; B.S. in Ed., Ed.M., Boston University; Columbia

Mary Isabel Caldwell . . . . Physical Education
B.S., University of Wisconsin; M.A., New York University; Boston University

E. Irene Graves . . . . Biology
B.A., Elmira College; M.A., Columbia; Cornell

Iva V. Lutz . . . . Methods
Gorham; B.S.E., M.A., Columbia

Gordon L. Reynolds . . . . Art; Supervision in Training School
Fine Arts Department; B.S. in Ed., Massachusetts School of Art; Columbia

Balfour S. Tyndall..Science; Geography
    B.A., University of Maine; Ed.M., Harvard
Ruth I. Low...English; Dramatic Club
    Salem; New England Conservatory of Music; Gallishaw School of Writing
William A. McGurren................................Chemistry; Physical Science
    B.A., Holy Cross; Clark; Boston College
Frederick A. Meier, Jr...Physical Education
    B.S., M.S., Boston College; Bridgewater
John L. Davoren..Education; Sociology
    B.L.I.; Emerson; Boston University; University of Alabama
Clement C. Maxwell..English; History
    A.B., Holy Cross; A.M., Ph.D., Fordham

The Training School

Martha M. Burnell..Principal
    Gorham; Bridgewater; Columbia
Neva I. Lockwood...Grade Six
    Bridgewater; Columbia; B.S., Boston University
Evelyn R. Lindquist..Grade Six
    B.S. in Ed., Bridgewater
Louise H. Borchers..Grade Five
    Fitchburg; Columbia; B.S., M.A., Boston University
A. Mabelle Warner..Grade Five
    Salem; Boston University
Katherine Packard..Grade Four
    B.S. in Ed., Bridgewater; Columbia
Helen E. Sleeper...Grade Four
    Castine; Boston University; Columbia
Lucy S. Braley...Grade Three
    Bridgewater; Boston University; American Institute of Normal Methods
Charlotte H. Thompson...Grade Three
    Fitchburg; Columbia; B.S., Boston University
Gladys L. Allen...Grade Two
    Machias; Farmington; Emerson
Gertrude M. Rogers...Grade Two
    Pratt Institute; Columbia; B.S., Boston University
Grace E. Smith..Grade One
    Symonds Kindergarten Training School; Boston University; Boston Teachers College
Mary L. Marks...Kindergarten
    Wheelock; Boston University

Administration

Bernice H. Geyer..Principal Clerk
Doris I. Hadley...Secretary
Kathleen M. Gebar..Clerk
Edna M. Mullen...Head Matron
Jean C. Haggart..Resident Nurse
Thomas E. Annis..Chief Engineer

REQUIREMENTS FOR ADMISSION
(Effective September, 1937)

I. Application for Admission. Every candidate for admission to a teachers college is required to fill out a blank entitled "Application for Admission to a State Teachers College" and send it to the president of the teachers college which he desires to enter. This blank may be secured from the principal of the high school or the teachers college and may be filed after January 1 of the candidate's senior year. The blank should be filed by June 1.

II. Blanks to be Filed by the High School Principal. The principal of the high school is expected to fill out two blanks—one giving the "High School Record" for each year, and the other a "Rating of Personal Characteristics"—and send them to the president of the teachers college.

III. General Qualifications. Every candidate for admission as a regular student must meet the following requirements:

1. Health. The candidate must be in good physical condition and free from any disease, infirmity, or other defect which would unfit him for public school teaching. A statement from the family physician and examination by the college physician are the required evidences of satisfactory health.

2. High School Graduation. The candidate must be a graduate of a standard four-year high school, or have equivalent preparation.

3. Completion of Fifteen Units of High School Work. The "High School Record" must show the completion of fifteen units accepted by the high school in meeting graduation requirements.

"A unit represents a year's study in any subject in a secondary school, so planned as to constitute approximately one-fourth of a full year of work for a pupil of normal ability. To count as a unit, the recitation periods shall aggregate approximately 120 sixty-minute hours. Time occupied by shop or laboratory work counts one-half as much as time in recitation."

4. Personal Characteristics. The "Rating of Personal Characteristics" and the moral character of the candidate must, in the judgment of the president of the teachers college, warrant the admission of the candidate.

IV. Scholarship Requirements. Of the 15 units presented for admission, 12 must be selected from the list given under 2, g. of this section and must include the 6 units named in this paragraph as "Prescribed." The additional 3 units required may consist of any work which the high school accepts as meeting its graduation requirements.

Prescribed (6 units):

English	3 units
American History and Civics	1 unit
Mathematics	1 unit
Science	1 unit

1. Certification

(a) The privilege of certification is extended to public and private schools and academies in the State of Massachusetts. The certificating grade is A or B (80-100). Units of certification will be determined on the same basis as units of credit, subject to the restrictions which follow.

Admission by certificate alone is granted to candidates who present work of certificating grade in 12 units as follows: six from the prescribed list and six others from the list given under 2, g. following. The number of units offered is subject to the restrictions of 2, f.

The Department of Education reserves the right to withdraw the privilege of certification from any institution when its students fail to measure up to the standards required by the Department. The responsibility of the high school will continue through the freshman year in the teachers colleges.

(b) In the case of subjects which continue for two years, the grade for the last year must be A or B in order that both units may be accepted for certification; if the subjects continue for three or four years, the grade for one other year, as well as the grade for the last year, must be A or B, in order that 3 or 4 units may be accepted for certification.

In the case of English, only 3 units will be accepted among the required 12 units. A fourth unit of English may be accepted as one of the 3 additional units.

2. Examination

(a) Any candidate whose record does not entitle him to certification for at least 5 units is required to secure credit by examination for 12 units of work.

(b) Any candidate who is a graduate of a high school not entitled to certification may be permitted to secure credit toward admission by passing examinations in subjects evaluating 10 units (prescribed, 6 units; additional, 4 units), provided the 5 other units necessary to make up the 15 units required for admission represent subjects which the high school accepts as meeting its graduation requirements and in which the candidate has secured grades acceptable to the high school.

(c) It is understood that candidates are not to present themselves for examination in subjects not pursued during the last four years of the secondary school.

(d) Preliminary examinations may be taken either in June or September by students who have completed the third year in a secondary school, in not more than 5 units, other than English.

(e) Subject to the admission conditions stated above, credits received in the College Entrance Board Examinations may be accepted for admission.

(f) The units must be so distributed that the number offered in any field, including the prescribed units, shall not be more than the following, with the provision that the minimum total amount in any field except Foreign Language shall be 1 unit: Social Studies, 4 units; Science, 3 units; Foreign Language, 4 units, no credit accepted for less than 2 units of any one language; Mathematics, 3 units; Commercial Subjects, 2 units; Fine and Practical Arts, 2 units.

(g) Examinations will be offered by the teachers colleges in the following subjects:

		Maximum Number of Units in Each Field
ENGLISH		
English Literature and Composition	3 units	3
SOCIAL STUDIES		
American History and Civics	1 unit	
Community Civics	½ or 1 unit	
History to about 1700	1 unit	
European History since 1700	1 unit	
Economics	½ or 1 unit	4
Problems of Democracy	½ or 1 unit	
Ancient History	1 unit	
English History	1 unit	
Medieval and Modern History	1 unit	
SCIENCE		
General Science	½ or 1 unit	
Biology or Botany or Zoology	½ or 1 unit	
Chemistry	1 unit	
Physics	1 unit	3
Physical Geography	½ or 1 unit	
Physiology and Hygiene	½ or 1 unit	
Astronomy or Geology	½ or 1 unit	

FOREIGN LANGUAGE

Latin................................. 2, 3, or 4 units ⎫
French............................... 2 or 3 units ⎪
Spanish.............................. 2 units ⎬
German.............................. 2 or 3 units ⎪
Italian............................... 2 or 3 units ⎭

MATHEMATICS

Algebra.............................. 1 or 2 units ⎫
Arithmetic........................... 1 unit ⎬ 3
Geometry............................ 1 unit ⎪
College Review Mathematics........... 1 unit ⎭

COMMERCIAL SUBJECTS

Stenography (including Typewriting)...... 1 or 2 units ⎫
Bookkeeping......................... 1 unit ⎬ 2
Commercial Geography................. ½ or 1 unit ⎪
Commercial Law...................... ½ or 1 unit ⎭

FINE AND PRACTICAL ARTS*

Home Economics...................... 1 unit ⎫
Manual Training...................... 1 unit ⎬ 2
Drawing............................. ½ or 1 unit ⎪
Music............................... 1 unit ⎭

*In these fields one additional unit may be granted as follows: in Home Economics, Manual Training, Drawing, and Music, to candidates applying respectively for admission to the household arts courses at Framingham, the practical arts course at Fitchburg, the teacher training course at the Massachusetts School of Art, and the music course at Lowell.

V. Method of Selection of Candidates in Case of an Excess of Applicants. If the number of applicants for admission is, on July 1, in excess of the number that the facilities of the teachers college will accommodate, the plan of admission as already stated will be somewhat modified. The scholarship record and the ratings of the personal characteristics of **all** applicants will be evaluated in accordance with the method stated below. Candidates will then be admitted in the order of their total scores until the capacity of the teachers college has been reached.

(a) Scholarship will be allowed 75 points for 15 units of work.

(b) Personality will be allowed 25 points.

As a basis of computing the total score from the scholarship record, as submitted by the high school principal, a mark of "A" will be given 5 points; "B" 4 points; "C" 3 points; "D" 2 points.

As a basis of computing the personality record, which includes ten characteristics exclusive of health, a mark of "Excellent" will be allowed 2½ points; "Good" 2 points; "Fair" 1½ points; "Poor" 1 point.

VI. Place, Time, and Division of Examination. Entrance examinations may be taken in June and September at any state teachers college (including the Massachusetts School of Art) at the convenience of the applicant. A candidate may take all the examinations at one time or divide them between June and September. It is to be understood, however, that the number of applicants admitted as a result of the September examinations is limited to the facilities of the teachers colleges. Permanent credit will be given for any units secured by examination or certification.

VII. Admission as Advanced Students. A graduate of a normal school or a college may be admitted as a regular or advanced student, under conditions approved by the Department.

SCHEDULE OF ENTRANCE EXAMINATIONS FOR 1937 AND 1938

June 3 and September 13, 1937
June 2 and September 12, 1938

(Candidates are required to register one-half hour before their first examination)

8:30–10:30   English Literature and Composition.

10:30–12:30   Latin; Commercial Subjects:

Latin
Stenography (including Typewriting)
Bookkeeping

Commercial Geography
Commercial Law

1:30– 4:30   Social Studies:

American History and Civics
Medieval and Modern History
Community Civics
History to about 1700
European History since 1700

Economics
Problems of Democracy
Ancient History
English History

June 4 and September 14, 1937
June 3 and September 13, 1938

8:30–10:30   Mathematics:

Algebra
Arithmetic

Geometry
College Review Mathematics

10:30–12:30   Modern Foreign Language:

French
Spanish

German
Italian

1:30– 3:30   Science:

General Science
Biology, Botany or Zoology
Chemistry
Physics

Physical Geography
Physiology and Hygiene
Astronomy
Geology

3:30– 5:00   Fine and Practical Arts:

Home Economics
Drawing

Manual Training
Music

EXTENSION COURSES

Since 1927, the State Teachers College, in affiliation with the State Department of University Extension, has offered credit courses of collegiate grade in order to provide for graduates of the two-year, three-year and four-year (without degree) curricula the opportunity of qualifying for the degree of Bachelor of Science in Education. Graduates of the two-year curriculum are required to pass satisfactorily courses aggregating thirty semester hours in addition to a year of work in residence. Graduates of the three-year curriculum are required to pass satisfactorily courses aggregating thirty semester hours. Graduates of the four-year curriculum (without degree) are required to pass satisfactorily courses aggregating fifteen semester hours.

The year in residence requires a minimum of thirty semester hours in approved courses taken in the teachers college from which the candidate is to receive the degree. This work may be done either during the academic year or in summer courses, during a period not to exceed five years prior to the award of the degree. A limited number of other required credits may be gained in approved collegiate or extension courses.

Detailed information will be furnished, upon application, at the office of the Teachers College.

EXPENSES

Semester Fee. There is an annual fee of $50. Of this amount $25 must be paid in September, before registration in classes, and $25 on February 1.

Board. Rates for board and room are established by the State Department of Education. The present annual rate is $300, payable promptly as follows, the first payment to be made before a room is assigned.

At the opening of the college year in September	**$90.00**
December 1	**70.00**
February 1	**70.00**
April 1	**70.00**

An extra proprotionate charge is made for board during the regular vacation periods.

Laundry work to the value of 50 cents a week is allowed on the regular price list; any excess of this amount is an extra charge.

A special laundry identification system is used, at a small initial expense (not exceeding one dollar) to each student.

Gymnasium Laundry Fee. All students participating in Physical Education Activities are required to pay an annual fee of $2 to meet the expense of laundering the bath towels used by them in the gymnasium. This fee is due at the opening of the college year.

All payments must be made strictly in advance, without the presentation of bills. A diploma is not granted until all bills are paid.

Other Expenses. Certain student enterprises which are supported by all the students are financed by means of the Student Activities Fee, which is payable at the beginning of each college year. This fee may vary from year to year, but is approximately $6.50 for women and $10 for men.

Students purchase their textbooks, writing materials, art materials, gymnasium outfit, and all supplies carried away for their future use.

The required gymnasium outfit for women, consisting of special uniform and shower equipment, costs approximately $14. Full description, with blanks for ordering, is sent out with notification of admission.

The required gymnasium outfit for men, consisting of special uniform of pants, sweatpants, and sweatshirt, is to be ordered on blanks which are sent out with notification of admission. The approximate cost is $4. Soccer shoes and other necessary articles may be secured after college opens.

Tuition. To residents of Massachusetts tuition is free. Residents of other states may be admitted upon payment of tuition at the rate of $250 a year, one-half of which amount is payable at the beginning of each half-year; provided that the admission of such students does not exclude or inconvenience residents of Massachusetts.

PECUNIARY AID

It has been the custom for several years for the Legislature to appropriate an annual sum, varying from $4,000 to $6,000, for allotment to the teachers colleges, to be given to students from Massachusetts who are unable, without assistance, to meet their expenses. Students who receive this aid are expected to render some service in return. Residents of Bridgewater are not eligible.

RESIDENCE HALLS

All women students who do not live at home are required to live in the dormitories. Exceptions to this rule may be made through the dean of women if a student wishes to live with relatives or to work for her room and board in some home approved by the college.

There are two residence halls for women on the campus. Woodward Hall has eighty-four double rooms and Tillinghast Hall has thirty-seven single rooms. The central dining room is located in Tillinghast Hall.

Each dormitory is heated by steam and lighted by electricity. In each there are attractive reception rooms as well as rooms set aside for general recreational purposes and for the enjoyment of the radio. STUDENTS ARE NOT ALLOWED TO USE RADIOS, ELECTRIC IRONS, OR COOKING EQUIPMENT IN THEIR ROOMS. Special rooms have been equipped to be used for laundry and kitchenette purposes.

Rooms in these halls are supplied with furniture, including mattresses, pillows, and rugs. Students are required to bring napkin ring, two clothes bags for laundry, bath mat, 36 inches by 24 inches, towels, window curtains, bureau covers, and bed covering for single beds. The bed covering should include a mattress cover, four sheets, 60 inches by 108 inches, three pillow cases, two pairs of blankets, a spread, a couch cover, and two couch pillows.

A reassignment of rooms is made at the end of each college year, preference in choice being given to those who have been longest in the college.

Candidates for admission who have applied for rooms in advance may select their rooms on the day preceding the opening of the college, after the initial payment of $90 at the Business Office. The order of choice is determined by lot.

Rooms for men are arranged for in private houses near the campus. Assignments are made by the dean of men only, from an approved list.

ABSENCE .

Regular and punctual attendance is required of every student. Each case of prolonged absence on account of illness is dealt with individually.

STUDENTS MUST NOT MAKE ARRANGEMENTS INVOLVING ABSENCE FROM ANY EXERCISE WITHOUT PREVIOUSLY OBTAINING PERMISSION, AND MUST RETURN PUNCTUALLY AFTER ANY RECESS OR VACATION. Those who are necessarily absent at any time must make up lost work promptly upon their return.

When a student finds it necessary to withdraw from the college, he must return any of its books or other property which he may have, and receive regular dismissal from the president; otherwise he must not expect to receive any indorsement from the college.

ALUMNI ASSOCIATION

In 1842, two years after the opening of the Bridgewater Normal School, a ."Convention" was called, "having as its object the meeting of the alumni and students of the school." In 1845, the Alumni Association was formed, and has flourished ever since. At the present time, out of a total of about 6,500 living graduates, it has approximately 2,500 active members.

A meeting of this Association is held every year,—biennially in June at the College, and the alternate years in the spring at a Boston hotel. These meetings, especially the one in Bridgewater, draw a large attendance. Bridgewater Clubs have also been formed in many localities.

Graduates, as individuals, and also as members of alumni groups, have shown continuous loyalty to the College by means of gifts and personal service.

CURRICULA

Elementary Teachers Course. A four-year course of study designed for students preparing to teach in the first six grades, and leading to the degree of Bachelor of Science in Education.

The Kindergarten-Primary Course is a division of the Elementary Teachers Course, with special emphasis on preparation for teaching in primary grades.

Junior-Senior High School Teachers Course. A four-year course of study designed for students preparing to teach in the junior or senior high school, and leading to the degree of Bachelor of Science in Education.

Elementary Curriculum
(Including Kindergarten-Primary)

COURSE NUMBER AND TITLE	CREDITS			
	1st Year	2nd Year	3rd Year	4th Year
Education				
1. Introduction to education............	3	...	...	...
2. The learning process...............	2	...	...	...
3. Techniques in elementary grades.....	...	2	...	...
4. Supervised student teaching in Training School.......................	...	...	7½	...
5. Supervised student teaching in Public Schools.......................	...	...	...	7½
6. Elementary school problems.........	...	...	2	...
7. Applied psychology...............	...	...	3	...
9. The elementary curriculum..........	...	...	...	1½
10. Educational measurements...........	...	...	...	3
13. History of education..............	...	...	2	...
15. Kindergarten theory and methods (for kindergarten-primary students).....	...	...	...	...
16. Philosophy of education.........	...	...	...	3
English				
1. Oral expression	3	...	...	...
2. Written composition				
3. Composition...................	...	3	...	...
7. Techniques in elementary reading....	...	2	...	...
9. Public speaking.................	...	...	2	...
20. American drama	...	3	...	...
21. The American novel				
Library 1. Use of the library..........	1	...	...	...
Fine and Practical Arts				
1a. Introduction to art................	2	...	...	...
1b. Introduction to art................	...	1	...	...
2. Elementary art..................	...	2	...	...
Handwriting				
1. Practice.......................	½	...	...	...
2. Blackboard writing and methods.....	...	½	...	...
Mathematics				
1. Fundamentals...................	2	...	...	...
2. The teaching of arithmetic.........	...	2	...	...
Music				
1. Elementary theory...............	2	...	...	...
3. Teaching music in elementary schools..	...	...	2	...
Physical Education				
1. Activities......................	2	...	...	...
2. Activities......................	...	2	...	...
3a. Activities.....................	...	...	1½	...
3b. Theory.......................	...	...	1½	...
Health Education 1. Personal and community health......................	2	...	...	...
Health Education 2. School health......	...	1½	...	...
Science				
1. General biology.................	3	...	...	...
6. Elementary school science..........	...	2	...	...
9. Physical science.................	...	2	...	...
Social Science				
1. Principles of geography............	2	...	...	...
2. Regional geography—West.........	...	2	...	...
3. Regional geography—East..........	...	...	2	...
7. Survey of civilization..............	3	...	...	...
10. American history for elementary teachers.......................	...	...	...	4½
12. Principles of sociology.............	...	2	...	...
15. Principles of economics............	...	...	2	...
Total credits in required courses..........	27½	27	25½	19½
Minimum requirement in elective courses....	6	5	6½	10½
Minimum total requirement...............	33½	32	32	30

COURSE NUMBER AND TITLE	CREDITS			
	1st Year	2d Year	3rd Year	4th Year
Education				
1. Introduction to education...........	3	...	...	...
2. The learning process...............	2	...	...	...
3. Techniques in elementary grades.....	...	2	...	...
4. Supervised student teaching in Training School........................	...	...	7½	...
5. Supervised student teaching in Public Schools.......................	...	...	...	7½
7. Applied psychology................	...	...	3	...
8. Techniques in junior high school.....	...	...	2	...
10. Educational measurements...........	...	...	...	3
11. Junior high school organization	...	...	...	1½
13. History of education...............	...	...	2	...
16· Philosophy of education............	...	...	...	3
English				
1. Oral expression }	3	...	...	...
2. Written composition				
3. Composition.....................	...	3	...	...
9. Public speaking...................	...	...	2	...
14. Drama..........................	...	3	...	...
Library 1. Use of the library..........	1	...	...	...
Fine and Practical Arts				
1a. Introduction to art...............	2	...	...	...
1b. Introduction to art...............	...	1	...	...
3. Application of representation and design elements.................	...	2	...	...
Handwriting				
1. Practice.........................	½	...	...	...
2. Blackboard writing and methods......	...	½	...	...
Mathematics				
1. Fundamentals....................	2	...	...	...
Music				
1. Elementary theory.................	2	...	...	...
Physical Education for Women				
1. Activities.......................	2	...	...	...
2. Activities.......................	...	2	...	...
3a. Activities.......................	...	...	1½	...
3b. Theory.........................	...	...	1½	...
Health Education 1. Personal and community health........................	2	...	...	...
Health Education 2. School health......	...	1½	...	...
Physical Education for Men				
5. Theory and activities..............	4	...	...	...
6. Theory and activities..............	...	3½	...	...
7. Theory and activities..............	...	...	3	...
Science				
1. General biology..................	3	...	...	...
9. Physical science..................	...	2	...	...
Social Science				
1. Principles of geography............	2	...	...	...
2. Regional geography—West.........	...	2	...	...
7. Survey of civilization..............	3	...	...	...
12. Principles of sociology.............	...	2	...	...
15. Principles of economics............	...	...	2	...
Total credits in required courses..........	27½	21	21½	15
Minimum requirement in elective courses....	6	11	10½	15
Minimum total requirement..............	33½	32	32	30

EDUCATION

Education 1. Introduction to Education. Miss Beal and Miss Pope.

This is an orientation and guidance course.

Part I deals with problems that arise upon entrance to college life and college methods of work; these include such matters as participation in college social life, self-direction in more mature methods of study, and wise use of opportunities offered for the development of initiative and leadership. Since teachers are expected to participate in the social and institutional life of their communities as well as to make intellectual and professional contacts, training is given in the amenities and social conventions required of a person in public service. In addition, attention is paid to the development of those personal qualifications which are essential to successful teaching.

Part II aims to give an overview of the field of education, preparing for the understanding of the professional purpose of a teacher training institution, and for the more specialized and detailed study in later courses. It includes the development of public education and the effects of various movements on the purposes and aims of education in a democratic society.

The following organization serves as a basis of study: (1) The School of Yesterday; (2) The School of Today; (3) The School of Tomorrow. Observation of school situations gives meaning to the discussions. First year. 18 weeks, 3 credits.

Education 2. The Learning Process. Mr. Hunt.

This is an introductory course in psychology dealing with the child as a reacting organism, aiming to show how he becomes adjusted to his environment and achieves some mastery of the skills, knowledge, and attitudes necessary for constructive participation in the life of the community of which he is a part.

It includes a study of (1) the nervous system; (2) the inherited nature of the child as expressed in reflexes, instincts, and emotions; (3) the conditioned reflex and the general process of conditioning as the physiological basis of learning; (4) the most widely recognized "laws of learning" extensively applied to the problems of teacher-planning and economical pupil-learning; (5) the building up of a set of "teaching guides."

First year. 18 weeks, 2 credits.

Education 3. Principles and Techniques of Teaching and Classroom Management in Elementary Grades. Miss Lutz.

The principles of the learning process developed in elementary psychology serve as a basis for this course. A comparative and analytical study of the principles of method with the underlying techniques is carried on by research, observation, discussion, and demonstration in the Training School.

The following techniques in the teaching process are considered as typical: choice, analysis, and organization of subject matter; types of lessons; methods of study; lesson plans; unit teaching; activity program; selection of materials and methods.

A study of the problems of classroom management including discipline is also made.

Second year. 18 weeks, 2 credits.

Education 4. Supervised Student Teaching in the Training School. Miss Beal, Supervisor.

The training school serves as a laboratory where students engage in the scientific study of children, and of teaching and learning situations as they are encountered in a modern elementary school.

As the study progresses, students participate in problems of increasing difficulty to the point where they can undertake the duties of the room teacher.

Conferences, readings, reports are required of all.

Third year. 9 weeks, 7½ credits.

Education 6. Elementary School Problems. Miss Lutz.

This course deals with modern trends in education; diagnosis and remedial work; types of school organization; criteria for judging procedures and method; visual education, and its place in the school's progress.

Group and individual reports of modern educational writings, texts, and professional books are required in this course. Third year. 18 weeks, 2 credits.

Education 7. Applied Psychology. Mr. Hunt.
This course is designed for students who have taken Education 2. It continues the study of the learning process with particular attention to the psychology of perceptual learning, memory, imagination, and problem solving. It deals especially with the processes by which the developing pupil may be successfully guided by his teachers in the acquisition of useful and accurate ideas—(1) directly, through the best kinds of first-hand contact with his environment, (2) indirectly, through the effective study of textbooks and other secondary means for securing the best possible understanding of the world at a distance and the life and events of other times.
The latter part of the course is devoted to a study of those aspects of mental hygiene most likely to be helpful to the student in understanding himself and in recognizing and preventing tendencies to maladjustment among his pupils. Third year. 18 weeks, 3 credits.

Education 8. Principles and Techniques of Teaching in the Junior High School. Miss Lutz.
This course deals with the principles which are basic to the junior high level with relation to methods of teaching. It considers the psychology of the learner, the organization of materials, standards of attainment, and the procedures by which these standards are developed.
Major emphasis is directed to the following topics: the curriculum of the junior high school; the learning possibilities of the ability ranges; selection and arrangement of subject matter; modification of teaching procedures for varying abilities; study of methods of study; assignments; problem solving, socialized recitation, and classroom organization and management. Third year. 18 weeks, 2 credits.

Education 13. History of Education. Mr. Davoren.
The scope of the course in History of Education includes: (1) a brief study of the present-day program of education in typical school systems; (2) the major theories and tendencies in modern education; (3) the major developments of our public school system; (4) the significant contributions made to education in thought and practice by European leaders; (5) the economic, industrial, and social influences which have aided or retarded educational progress.
Reports, assigned readings, and class discussions are required of each student. Third year. 18 weeks, 2 credits.

Education 15. Kindergarten Theory and Methods. Miss Marks.
A study of the origin, evolution, and growth of the kindergarten, including its aims, ideals, values, requirements; life and influence of Froebel, Pestalozzi, Montessori, and others; present status of the kindergarten in the United States; and influence upon the kindergarten of the changing conceptions of education.
A part of the course is devoted to the study of play materials for young children, traditional and modern; industrial arts and the methods of using materials; and a program for the well-rounded school life of the kindergarten child.
This course parallels practice teaching in kindergarten; thus time is spent in discussing actual classroom situations as they arise during this training period.
Credits are included with those of Education 4.

Education 17. Directed Observation in the Kindergarten and Primary Grades. (Elective.) Miss Beal and Training School Faculty.
The purpose of this course is to study (1) the educational objectives of the kindergarten and primary grades, and (2) the importance of the kindergarten as a basis for the growth and development of children in the primary grades. Third year. 18 weeks, 2 credits.

Education 5. Supervised Student Teaching in the Public Schools. Miss Beal, Supervisor.

This period provides opportunities in the public schools for continuous experience in all classroom activities under regular classroom conditions. Experience is gained in the study of individual differences, teaching techniques, and effective school management. Supervision is given by the classroom teacher and members of the college staff.

Conferences, readings, reports are required of all.

Fourth year. 9 weeks, 7½ credits.

Education 9. The Elementary Curriculum. Miss Lutz.

This course includes a consideration of problems relating to the curriculum of the elementary school; the principles of curriculum construction; the process of curriculum making and revision; the bearing of current social factors on curriculum construction; the procedure for setting up objectives, guiding principles, course of study units, and units of instruction; significant educational points of view and their application to curriculum making; and the contribution of research and experimental studies to the selection and arrangement of materials in the curriculum.

Recent courses of study prepared by public and private schools, as well as abstracts of research and experimental investigations in various fields, are used as illustrative material for this course. Fourth year. 9 weeks, 1½ credits.

Education 10. Tests and Measurements. Mr. Hunt.

Introductory study of the great range in ability within the typical school grade, the meaning of general intelligence, and the causes of the great range in ability to learn. Study of the development of the modern science of intelligence testing. Work of Binet, and the Terman revision of the Binet scale for use in America. Training in the use of the revised scale in the measurement of the intelligence of children of school age, computing IQ's, and interpreting them for a better understanding of the individual pupil's power to work successfully in school.

Study of the best known group-tests of mental ability and of achievement in the major subjects of instruction. Training in the use of statistical methods of handling the data resulting from such tests and interpreting the same. Diagnostic and remedial activities based on testing. Technique in the construction of tests by the teacher to more scientifically measure the success of her own instruction. Fourth year. 18 weeks, 3 credits.

Education 11. Junior High School Organization. Mr. Hunt.

This course is planned to provide a general understanding of the junior high school as an important part of the present-day scheme of public school education. It includes (1) a brief study of the period of adolescence, a survey of the changing concepts in the psychology of that period, with conclusions as to the influence which a knowledge of adolescence should exert on the methods of instruction and control of the early adolescent. Aims and characteristics of a school in which the majority of pupils are pubescent or definitely adolescent. A survey of the strong and weak points of departmental instruction. Needs for educational guidance and for the beginning of exploration of vocational aptitudes to the end that each pupil may be gradually directed toward the career for which he is best adapted. A survey of the advantages and difficulties of homogeneous classification of pupils, different methods of marking, constructive use of reports to parents, promotion problems, and the administration of extra-curricular activities. If time, a unit of work is included on the making of the junior high school program. Fourth year. 9 weeks, 1½ credits.

Education 16. Philosophy of Education. Mr. Davoren.

The major purposes of the course in philosophy of education are to provide the student opportunities to further organize his educational ideas, learnings, and understandings into workable wholes in order that he may make as sane a start as possible in teaching; to guide the student in his "thinking through" educational problems to the end that he will make the optimum use of clear thinking, the scientific spirit, research, and reason in all matters of education; to encourage in the student a wider and a more significant understanding of the relation between the learner and the teacher; to enlarge opportunities for the further development of a wholesome philosophy of teaching.

As means to ends in developing a more scientific and a more workable student point of view, problems arising from the following relationships are presented and studied: the significance of tradition in a program of education; the significance of progress in a program of education: the application of the spirit of research to the field of education; the responsibilities and obligations of members of the teaching profession; education in relation to a democratic form of government.

Reports, assigned readings, class discussions, and simple problems in research are required of each student.

The course is presented by means of lectures, directed study, group discussions, and illustrations from selected materials and references.　　　　Fourth year.　27 weeks, 3 credits.

ENGLISH

English 1.　Oral Expression.　Miss Low.

The purpose of this course is as follows: (1) to train students in proper use of voice as a medium of teaching; (2) to develop poise; (3) to acquaint students with stories and story-telling.

The required work includes (1) recitation and oral reading of selections; (2) original descriptions; (3) impersonations; (4) story-telling; reading and discussion of books; selection, narration, illustration, and dramatization of stories; preparation of a story-hour.

Credits are included with those of English 2.

English 2.　Written Composition.　Miss Low.

The aim of this course is to enable the student to increase the effectiveness of his written expression. In all the work covered, stress is laid upon ability to select and express essential meaning with clarity and accuracy. The course is correlated with the course in Oral Expression, so that analysis and written composition are often based upon material, such as literary selections, reports, and speeches, also used for vocal interpretation.

The following technical material illustrates the content of the course. Organization: Precis and paraphrases, outlines, letters, reports, brief essays. Sentences: Simple analysis, correct usage, rhetorical effectiveness. Vocabulary: Enlargement and increased accuracy in the use of words.

The work is carried on by means of class discussions, frequent short assignments, and individual conferences. Students showing a mastery of the fundamentals of composition may be permitted to take up some more advanced phase of English.

English 1 and 2.　First year.　18 weeks, 3 credits.

English 3.　Composition.　Miss Lovett and Miss Low.

This course has the following aims: skill in speaking and writing; training in thinking, through the discussion of essays dealing with modern problems, and through voluntary writing substituted for regular assignments.

Teaching materials are, in the main, selected according to the needs of the class. Much opportunity is offered for informal debating, application of the principles of rhetoric, paraphrasing, precis writing, and the writing of term papers.

Second year.　18 weeks, 3 credits.

English 4a.　Problems of Teaching English in Junior High School.　(Elective.)　Miss Lovett.

This course presents a point of view with respect to the "materials" of English taught in the more progressive junior high schools. A short survey is given, showing the principles of grammar with practice in analysis, the place of grammar as a school subject, the methods of organizing the subject, and the relationship of grammar to composition. Individual research, practice in writing and in presentation, in the planning of assignments and long units, in the conduct of recitations, and in testing and grading are included. Other subjects examined are letter writing, vocabulary study, extra-curricular English activities, illustrative materials and methods, and debating.　　　　Credits are included with those of English 4b.

English 4b.   History of the English Language.   (Elective.) Miss Lovett.

This course deals with the place of English in the modern world and with its relationships to other languages, ancient and modern. It is intended to help the student deal with the problems of language that arise in the teaching of English and to establish standards for criticism. The course gives the historical background of the English language and describes related social and literary movements that have affected the development of our language. English is shown to be flexible, changing, and subject to popular influence. Stress is laid upon diction, dictionary study, and the development of standards of correct usage.

English 4a and 4b.   Third year.   27 weeks, 4½ credits.

English 22.   Creative Writing.   (Elective.) Miss Lovett.

This course is intended for people interested in any form of creative composition. The aim of the course is to teach the student the fundamentals of clear and effective expression through the study of types of writing. There is a required minimum of accomplishment established for each semester's work, but each student may select his own activities.

Third year.   27 weeks, 4½ credits.

English 5.   Journalistic Writing.   (Elective.) Miss Lovett.

This is a laboratory course in writing. The aims are those of "good composition"; namely, clearness, conciseness, correctness, and coherence. The models used are such as are found in the leading newspapers and periodicals. The principal types of news stories are studied, and examples are collected and criticized. The student is given considerable practice in original writing with much emphasis upon revision.

Individual research is provided to develop skill in the reading and the judging of newspapers. The student is prepared to guide pupils in the intelligent reading and use of newspapers, and to plan and manage school newspapers.

Credits are included with those of English 6.

English 6.   Teaching of English in Junior and Senior High Schools.   (Elective). Miss Lovett.

This is a seminar course intended for the students who are majoring in English. Such subjects as the following may be selected: creative writing, versification, grammar, the possible relationships of literature and composition, the use of standard tests. The student formulates the results of his study for presentation to the group.

English 5 and 6.   Fourth year.   27 weeks, 4½ credits.

English 7·   Techniques in Elementary Reading. Miss Davis.

The purposes of this course are as follows: to acquaint students (1) with the most outstanding problems that arise in the teaching of reading in the elementary grades; and (2) with general and specific procedures in this field. The course also deals with the teaching of other language arts, where they correlate with the teaching of reading.

The required work includes (1) observation and discussion of reading activities, (2) assigned readings in texts and manuals, comparing and evaluating material; (3) acquaintance with the practical use of tests and supplementary materials; and (4) examination and evaluation of modern procedures and texts in the field of language and spelling in the elementary grades.

Second year.   18 weeks, 2 credits.

English 17.   Problems in the Teaching of Reading and the Language Arts.   (Elective). Miss Davis.

This course deals much more fully than does English 7 with the problems and sources of information in the field of the language arts. It is not a repetition of English 7, but aims to give students a wide and somewhat detailed acquaintance with available modern texts and the results of research. As far as practicable, the course is carried on by directed individual and group study.

The course is organized around (1) one or two class texts, for unification, and (2) a series of problems. These problems are proposed by the instructor or by the class, are formulated in class discussion, and are assigned to a group for intensive study, while the remainder of the class does general reading on the same topic or works out some practical application. The group then reports its findings to the class, for discussion and further study.

In this way students become familiar with sources of information, discuss many aspects of reading and teaching, pursue (to a limited extent) individual and group research, work out illustrative and typical procedures, and systematize the whole for future reference and use.

Third year. 27 weeks, 4½ credits.

English 18. Remedial Reading. (Elective). Miss Davis.

The membership of this course is limited to a designated number of students who wish to do extensive work in the field of Remedial Reading. These students must be willing and able to give considerable outside time and self-directed effort to the problems involved. In admitting students to the course the advisers give preference to students who have already shown, either in English or in practice teaching, an aptitude for this kind of work.

The course includes extensive readings in books and magazine articles using Gates' **Improvement of Reading** as a basal book, with supplementary reading in Betts' **Prevention and Correction of Reading Difficulties,** McCallister's **Remedial and Corrective Instruction in Reading,** Harrison's **Reading Readiness,** and others both old and new.

A definite program of remedial work with recommended children is carried out, by means of case studies, tests, and individual teaching. Each student gives from two to four hours each week, during parts of the course, to such directed work.

Informal class and individual conferences clarify and unify the work of the course.

Fourth year. 27 weeks, 4½ credits.

English 11. Current Literature. (Elective). Miss Lovett.

This is primarily a reading course intended to give students an opportunity for an extensive, exploratory survey of modern literature. The short story, the novel, the drama, poetry, the essay, biography, and popular books dealing with the sciences, economics, sociology are presented. Assignments or readings and reports are prepared by the students for themselves, with advice as to suitability given by the instructor. The amounts of reading are adjusted to the students' ability. First year. 36 weeks, 4 credits.

English 19. Introduction to World Literature. (Elective). Miss Lovett.

This course offers students with reading ability an opportunity to become familiar with the work of some of the best-known authors in European literature from Homer to the modern Russian writers. It is not a survey course nor a study of literary types.

Students are encouraged to follow their own tastes in their outside reading and to develop the habit of reading and self-directed intensive study apart from this or other courses, as a key to future education.

The authors studied are listed for two semesters in order that students may enroll for the course for two years without repetition of subject matter.

First or second year. 18 weeks, 3 credits.

English 12. Survey of English Literature. (Elective). Dr. Maxwell.

This survey course attempts to co-ordinate and arrange the student's knowledge and thinking by class study of important pieces of literature for their intrinsic value, and for their social significance.

The organization is loosely chronological. Relatively unproductive periods are studied briefly, in order that the few masterpieces may be enjoyed, and tendencies noted. The richer literary periods are studied more in detail, with special mention of about twenty major poets, essayists, and novelists, and the significance of the work of each.

The method of the course includes lectures, discussions, outside reading, and oral and written reports. Historical and social backgrounds are presented briefly by the instructor or by students. One period is made the subject of simple directed research on the part of the class, concluded by a test. For this research, outlines, problems, instruction, and supervision are furnished. Credits are included with those of English 13.

English 13. Survey of American Literature. (Elective). Dr. Maxwell.

This course attempts to show and to explain the various stages in the development of our national literature. Major emphasis is placed upon the literature of the nineteenth and twentieth centuries, showing the effects of European culture, growing nationalism, liberalization of thought, movements of peoples, and industrialism.

Since New England prose and poetry are so commonly studied in the public schools, they furnish the important materials for this course in order that students may have an intelligent background for teaching. The chief authors of other regions are also stressed. The class discusses miscellaneous modern literature, expressing individual reactions, and formulating simple standards of criticism.   English 12 and 13.   Second year.   36 weeks, 6 credits.

English 14. Drama and Dramatics. Miss Hill.

Reading and study of chief contemporary dramatists of Europe, Great Britain, and America. This course takes up a study of plays as "the abstract and brief chronicles of the time"; a study of dramatic technique and of play production; discussion of current plays; discussion of problems of stage management, committee work, lighting, costuming, make-up, character interpretation. Presentation of plays by members of class when program permits.

Second year.   18 weeks, 3 credits.

English 20. The American Novel. Miss Hill.

This course offers a survey of the work of American novelists, pioneers and artists, from 1798 to the present day; historical and critical consideration of novels presenting our national, regional, political, economic, and social life of more than a century; the development of this literary form from prose tale, character essay and short story to the contemporary novel of scope and distinction in materials and craftsmanship.

Credits are included with those of English 21.

English 21. American Drama. Miss Hill.

This course offers a study of representative American plays and of the development of the American stage from Colonial days to the present; the motives, the interests, and the changing standards underlying the history and development of the theatre in America; national development as reflected in dramatic forms; the commercial, provincial, and experimental theatres; civic, cultural, and spiritual values of drama approached from the viewpoints of the speech arts rather than from the angle of analytic study of dramatic form; oral reading and interpretation.

English 20 and 21.   Second year.   18 weeks, 3 credits.

English 9. Public Speaking. Miss Low.

This course deals with practice in platform speaking: speech improvement; preparing teachers to speak clearly and effectively in classroom, assembly, open forum, or public meetings, out-of-doors speaking. The material used for study includes problems in communication of simple ideas; interviews, discovering unique viewpoints and novel reactions of other people on interesting questions; reports to the class; platform deportment.

Practice is given in Unison Speech, and training in the leading of Verse Choirs, in connection with a study of this movement in Europe, England, and America.

The course gives a minimum of theory, with a maximum of practice.

Third year.   18 weeks, 2 credits.

English 15a. The Modern Novel. (Elective). Miss Hill.

In this course the following topics are considered: a survey of the novel since Scott; the importance of the novel in the interpretation of contemporary life; the craft of the novelist; analysis and comparison of novels in accordance with the accepted standards of criticism; promotion of good taste in the reading of fiction; cultivation of the habit of rapid reading of fiction; special attention given to such writers as Dickens, Eliot, Hardy, Meredith. Required reading: ten contemporary novels.   Credits are included with those of English 15c.

English 15b. Nineteenth Century Prose and Poetry. (Elective). Miss Hill.

In this course the following topics are considered: interpretation of the work of representative poets, including Tennyson, Browning, Arnold, Morris, Swinburne, Meredith,

Hardy; the art, music, and diction of Victorian poetry; the Victorian reaction to the world of nature, color, sound, and shape; the spiritual significance of nineteenth century literature. Required readings in prose: Coleridge, Lamb, Hazlitt, Newman, Ruskin, Arnold, Huxley, Pater, Stevenson.   Credits are included with those of English 15c.

English 15c.   Modern American and British Poetry.   (Elective).   Miss Hill.
In this course the following topics are considered: a study of the chief modern poets, schools of poetry; interpretations of modern life; the changed attitudes toward the common life; changes in theme, form, and poetic diction in the new poetry; Emily Dickinson, Robinson, Frost, Sandburg, Stevenson, Housman, Masefield, and others.
English 15a, 15b, and 15c.   Third year.   27 weeks, 4½ credits.

English 8.   Dramatics.   (Elective).   Miss Low.
The purposes of this course are as follows: (1) to enable students to meet the practical educational problems found in presenting assembly programs, and forming and directing junior and senior high school dramatic clubs; (2) to improve the ability of the student in the interpretation and the presentation of dramatic literature.
The required work includes (1) the study and discussion of a text on play production; (2) study of vocal and pantomimic expression; (3) reading and written reports of five one-act plays a week; (4) study of the development of the drama,—preparing a theme on some phase of the drama; (5) preparation and presentation of typical assembly programs; (6) coaching and presenting two one-act plays; (7) class study of one Shakespeare play; and (8) writing a one-act play.   Fourth year.   27 weeks, 4½ credits.

English 16b.   Twelve Plays of Shakespeare.   (Elective).   Miss Hill.
This is a course in reading and appreciation; a study of the plays **as plays;** a study of the philosophy of the poet-dramatist. Six of the twelve plays are selected for vocal interpretation.
Such plays as the following are selected: Henry IV, pt. 1; Henry IV, pt. 2; Henry V; Julius Caesar; Antony and Cleopatra; Hamlet; Othello; Romeo and Juliet; Coriolanus; The Winter's Tale; The Tempest.   Credits are included with those of English 16d.

English 16c.   Literary Criticism.   (Elective).   Miss Hill.
This course offers opportunity for oral and written criticism expressing "the reaction of the literary material upon the reader's taste and spiritual susceptibility"; a study of best contemporary criticism; criticism as literature; individual problems in the criticism of current biographies, autobiographies, novels, poems, and plays.
Credits are included with those of English 16d.

English 16d.   Ancient Drama.   (Elective).   Miss Hill.
This course offers a study of the evolution of the drama from religious ritual to the vigorous dramatic expression of the great Greek, Latin, and Oriental playwrights; reflection of racial and national distinctions and peculiarities in plays of historic and intrinsic values; significant moments in the pageant of civilization caught, emphasized and interpreted by creative and critical geniuses of ancient races; presentation of plays as dramatic masterpieces rather than as drill material for literary training.   Such plays as the following are read: "Antigone", Sophocles; The Captives", Plautus; "Sakoontala"; "Kalidasa"; the "Noh Plays" of Japan.
English 16b, 16c, and 16d.   Fourth year.   27 weeks, 4½ credits.

Library 1.   Introduction to the Use of the Library.   Miss Carter.
· This course gives a general introduction to the use of libraries, with emphasis on the use of the Teachers College Library. The subjects covered are the main divisions of the Dewey Decimal classification; arrangement of the library; leading dictionaries; encyclopedias; the card catalog; magazine indexes; reference books in specific fields, such as the following: "Living Authors", Brewer's "Readers' Handbook", Harper's "Dictionary of Classical Literature", "Pageant of America"; the making of simple bibliographies; book selection aids, such as "U. S. Catalog", "Book Review Digest."   First year.   18 weeks, 1 credit.

Library 2. Literature for Elementary Grades. (Elective). Miss Carter.

    Children's books are considered for their appeal to an adult intelligence as well as to the minds of children. The topics covered are the following: illustrators and illustrations of children's books; Mother Goose, its place in literature; first interests in reading; folk literature of many lands; children's poetry; modern writers of fairy tales; fiction for the elementary grades; books in special fields, both fiction and non-fiction, such as animal books, books on Indians, geography, or science; methods and devices to arouse interest in books. In connection with this course, work is done at the library desk, and book displays are planned for the Training School Library.   Second year. 36 weeks, 6 credits.

Library 3. Books for the Junior High School Library. (Elective). Miss Carter.

    The reading interests of upper elementary grades and junior high school are considered. The work includes the following: juvenile editions of Greek and Norse mythology; retold versions of national epics, legends, and romances, such as King Arthur, Robin Hood, The Mabinogian, Roland, Paul Bunyan; fiction, grouped by subjects, such as adventure stories, school stories, "series" books, and informational books.

    A study is made of the elementary school library, its organization and equipment. Practice work is given in the Training School Library, and in making book exhibits for the main library.   Third year. 27 weeks, 4½ credits.

Library 4. School Library Techniques. (Elective). Miss Carter.

    This course is designed to meet the needs of those students who have a mature interest in many types of books,—those valuable to both teachers and children for study and recreation,—and also an interest in the ways in which books are made available through the library, especially the school library.

    In the course students come in contact with very many books, new and old, juvenile and adult. They work among these books, examine lists, and see texts and reference books in many fields. Definite periods are reserved for book discussions and evaluations. Various projects in book-exploration are carried out.

    On the technical side, the administration of a school library is taken up, as to size, equipment, supervision, scheduling, and book selection. In the interests of proper professional procedure and accuracy, considerable time is spent upon simple cataloging, and Dewey Decimal classification. Practice is given in desk-work, guidance, and classification.

    A student who has made the best use of the opportunities offered should be able to conduct, or to help in the organization of, a school library.   Fourth year. 27 weeks, 4½ credits.

FINE AND PRACTICAL ARTS

Art 1a. Introduction to Art. Miss Nye.

    This course aims to arouse interest in the need of art expression as a preparation for teaching. Through the use of line, form, color, and pattern, students learn to express ideas and represent familiar forms as the circumstances of teaching may require. Students also learn principles and techniques while developing the habit of thoughtful observation, and the recognition of beauty.

    In this course the following fundamentals are considered:

    In representation, the development of power to create sketches of typical scenes of everyday life in water-color, crayons, etc.;

    In lettering, the application of well-spaced Gothic letters to simple objects in common use;

    In color, (1) its enjoyment in both art and nature, (2) establishment of correct terminology, and (3) development of knowledge of tone relations through the study of informal scales;

    In design, (1) through the study of slides and pictures the realization that design is orderly arrangement, (2) the recognition and enjoyment of the laws of order, and (3) the application of these laws in free brush patterns to simple objects for personal and school use.   First year. 18 weeks, 2 credits.

Art 5. Blockprinting. (Elective). Miss Nye.

Various problems suggested by the life of the student, such as monograms, place and greeting cards, calendars, surface patterns, and illustrations are created and then worked out in the medium of block-printing.

Simple one color blocks are designed at first, the class progressing to a two and three color print.   First year.   36 weeks, 4 credits.

Art 11. Practical Arts. Woodworking. Printing. (Elective).

The purpose of the course is to give to the student practical experience in a number of lines of useful handwork that a teacher can direct and supervise.

Woodworking: Articles are made that are required for school use, toys, repair work on school and home equipment.

Principles of Printing: This section of the course establishes orderly procedure in practical shopwork in printing. Extensive practice is given in printing, with use of foot and power press. The work in printing offers an excellent opportunity for correlation with certain activities in other departments of the college.   First year.   36 weeks, 2 credits.

Admission by special permission only.

Art 2. Elementary Art. Mr. Reynolds.

In this course the student is provided with the opportunity to develop his creative abilities in representation, design, and color. A variety of problems are presented, which closely relate to school, home, and community activities. Various mediums are used, in order that the student may understand and more thoroughly present an integrated program.

Second year.   18 weeks, 2 credits.

Art 1b. Introduction to Art. Miss Nye.

This course builds directly upon that of the Freshman year. The purposes of the course are to develop, in the student, the ability to think in three dimensions; to acquaint him with the fundamental processes of handwork possible for school use; to develop skill in the handling of a few simple tools; and to develop creative power enough to design and construct good looking as well as correct and useful objects and articles for which the student finds need in school and home.   Second year.   18 weeks, 1 credit.

Art 3. Application of Representation and Design Elements. Mr. Reynolds.

The opportunity to develop creative ability is also presented in this course. A well-rounded background in art fundamentals and mediums is given to the student, in order that he may readily assume responsibilities in the modern school. Problems such as illustrations, decorative compositions, posters, decorative maps, and shadowgraphs are included.

Second year.   18 weeks, 2 credits.

Art 8. Handwork. (Elective). Miss Nye and Mr. Reynolds.

The student has an opportunity in this course to try out many mediums, working individually and with groups. Using a variety of tools, the student is encouraged to create problems that are closely related to differing age and class levels. Pottery, weaving, toys, model vehicles, buildings, etc., are constructed to satisfy a personal need or to establish a basis for planning an integrated program.   Second year.   36 weeks, 3 credits.

Adaptation and Application **Conferences.** Mr. Reynolds.

This course is offered during the period of practice teaching under direct supervision in the Training School. It provides the opportunity for the development of lesson plans in art and handwork, demonstrations of practical problems, and group discussions.

It acquaints the student with the aims and purposes of art courses as pursued in elementary and junior high schools, the results hoped for, and the standards by which these are to be judged. It demonstrates that the same approach used in teaching other subjects can be employed in teaching art.

It gives students as much experience as possible in utilizing other subjects and activities of the school to motivate the art lesson. Consideration of proper balance and emphasis on art interests for each grade and their relation to units of work are studied.

Credits are included with those of Education 4.

Art 4a and 4b. History of the Minor Arts and Art Appreciation. (Elective). Miss Nye and Mr. Reynolds.

History of the Minor Arts. This course guides the student to understand the forces behind the inventions and creations of man down through the centuries. He discovers that this ability to design and invent raised man above all other living beings. Special consideration is given to the functionalism of the many weapons, utensils, kinds of clothing, pottery, ornaments, etc., which served man and gave him joy. Modern industrial design takes on new meaning.

Appreciation. This course aims to advance the growth of the student in the enjoyment of beauty and the recognition of common sense principles in his surroundings. The selection of costume according to the coloring and type of the individual is discussed. Various problems in the choice of wall-papers, rugs, furniture, lamps, and their arrangement in the modern home are solved. Flowers are arranged according to principles of nature and design to bring out their particular beauty, and advice is exchanged on containers. Various school and civic problems in art are discussed in an effort to make the students alive to the function of art in their everyday lives. Third year. 27 weeks, 3 credits.

Art 9. Bookbinding. (Elective). Miss Nye.

Starting with sheets of paper, cardboard, and strips of leather, the student designs the size and coloring, applies pattern to either the cover or lining papers with finger paint, block print, or batik, chooses leather to harmonize, sews and binds her book for some particular use. The book may be sewed on tapes, sunken cords, or raised cords.

Third year. 27 weeks, 2¼ credits.

Art 6a. History of Art. (Elective). Mr. Reynolds.

A study of the history of art acquaints students with the most significant development of architecture, sculpture and painting through the ages, with references to parallel historical activities.

Through reading, visits to museums, observation and discussion of pictures, and lantern slides, the continuity and variation of traditions in fine arts are traced. A brief study of the environment, living conditions, and the aesthetic significance of each period (Prehistoric, Egyptian, Oriental, Greek, Roman, Renaissance, French 19th century, and Modern) and of great individuals is presented.

The student should gain a desire for further knowledge and a greater appreciation of both the fine and minor arts as an expression of the life of the people producing them. The arts at their height, in the various civilizations, are compared with modern contributions from those districts. Fourth year. 27 weeks, 3 credits.

Art 10. Advanced Handicrafts. (Elective). Miss Nye and Mr. Reynolds.

The students create their own designs and work them out in various mediums such as clay, papier-mache, cloth, plaster of Paris, leather, etc., producing many articles—marionettes, masks, pottery, pocket-books, hand-woven scarfs, and batiks.

Fourth year. 27 weeks, 3 credits.

HANDWRITING

Handwriting 1. Practice in Handwriting. Mr. Doner.

The aim in this course is to train all students to write a plain, fluent hand, so that by their own skill and example they will be prepared, as teachers, to teach others to write well. This involves study and practice in motor skill, quality of results, and speed. To accomplish these ends one class period and one hour of outside practice each week are the minimum requirements. The Correlated Handwriting Method is used, which means that all writing, in order to function as it should, must correlate with all other subjects.

First year. 18 weeks, ½ credit.

Handwriting 2. Blackboard Writing and Methods. Mr. Doner.

In this course the students devote considerable time to the practice and improvement of their blackboard writing. For the teacher, good plain blackboard writing is not only a necessity but a duty which she owes to her pupils. This course also provides some discussion of current methods of teaching this subject, including measurements and grading of handwriting. Second year. 18 weeks, ½ credit.

Handwriting 3. Advanced Practice. (Elective). Mr. Doner.
This course is for those students who wish to perfect their own plain, fluent handwriting. Any student desiring to specialize in the teaching or supervising of penmanship is encouraged to take this course. Training in student teaching is provided.
Third year. 27 weeks, ¾ credit.

Handwriting 4. Lettering. (Elective). Mr. Doner.
A course in Old English Lettering and Engrosser's Script Writing is offered to a limited number of students who are especially interested in the artistic and the beautiful. This work is not only attractive for decorative purposes in the schoolroom, but consists of styles appropriate for place cards, book covers, holiday greetings, engrossing names and courses on certificates, diplomas, etc. Fourth year. 27 weeks, ¾ credit.

MATHEMATICS

The following courses are offered because a study of the science of mathematics is one of the important means through which those who are to teach may become well-educated men and women. A teacher of mathematics needs to be inspired with mathematics. For his work as a teacher he needs to have strengthened certain concepts, skills, and knowledges which he already possesses; in addition, he needs to gain new concepts, wider knowledges, and deeper understanding in the field. These courses offer the best means for reaching the desired goal. For instance, for formula work trigonometry serves the purpose; for graph work, analytical geometry; for the concept of the function, calculus.

Mathematics 1. Fundamentals of Mathematics. Mr. Durgin.
Organization of the knowledge needed by teachers of Arithmetic. The course is designed to emphasize professionalized subject matter to such an extent that beginning teachers will have a wider field of knowledge, a surer conception of arithmetic, and a keener sense of values. First year. 18 weeks, 2 credits.

Mathematics 4. Trigonometry. (Elective). Mr. Durgin.
Trigonometric functions of any angle; solution of right triangles; logarithms; solution of general triangles; solution of trigonometric equations. This course is open to those students who have had a course in trigonometry as well as those who have not had such a course. Students with previous training in trigonometry will find this course profitable because of the use of practical applications, such as are found in surveying and astronomy.
Credits are included with those of Mathematics 5.

Mathematics 5. College Algebra. (Elective). Mr. Durgin.
This course covers the following topics: quadratic equations; progressions; variation; logarithms; compound interest and annuities; binomial theorem; functions; theory of equations; permutations and combinations; probability and determinants.
Mathematics 4 and 5. First year. 36 weeks, 6 credits.

Mathematics 2. The Teaching of Arithmetic. Miss Lutz.
This course follows Mathematics 1. It is designed to coordinate the previous year's work with a knowledge of methods needed for teaching. Emphasis is placed on teaching procedure. An analysis is made of some textbooks and courses of study. Some time is devoted to problems and projects in arithmetic, to the grading of drill material, standardized and diagnostic tests. Second year. 18 weeks, 2 credits.

Mathematics 6. Analytic Geometry. (Elective). Mr. Durgin.
Cartesian coordinates; loci problems; the straight line; the circle; polar coordinates; conic sections. This course is designed to enlarge, enrich, and coordinate the ideas of algebra

and geometry, and to promote the more effective teaching of both subjects. Stress is laid on ability to analyze a problem logically as distinguished from ability to manipulate formulas.
Second year. 36 weeks, 6 credits.

Mathematics 8. Differential and Integral Calculus. (Elective). Mr. Durgin.
Textbook: "Osgood's Introduction to the Calculus."
Third year. 27 weeks, 4½ credits.

Mathematics 3. Teaching of Mathematics in the Junior High School. (Elective). Mr. Durgin.
This course includes the methods of teaching topics in arithmetic, algebra, intuitive geometry, and numerical trigonometry, which are given in the junior high school. How the curriculum is determined, objectives to be attained, and the place of tests are discussed. Materials are collected to enrich the course of study. Permission of the instructor must be obtained for entrance to this course.
Fourth year. 27 weeks, 4½ credits.

MODERN LANGUAGES

French courses are elective, and open to those who have had three years of high school French or its equivalent. Teaching candidates in this field are required to elect all courses.

French 1. French for Cultural Purposes. Miss Bradford.
This course offers an opportunity to develop to the point of enjoyment the ability to read the foreign language, an ability approximating that in the mother tongue.
It stresses the ability to grasp readily, through reading, thought expressed in the foreign language. It includes the attainment of a reasonably fluent and accurate pronunciation for oral purposes, and skill in understanding the spoken language through the ear. It subordinates analytic grammar to the essentials of functional grammar.
The means to be employed are extensive and intensive reading of standard fourth-year texts and a text on French civilization; continuous oral-aural training in the form of summaries, reports, and discussion; phonetics.
First year. 36 weeks, 6 credits.

French 2. Correlated French. Miss Bradford.
The aim of the course is to correlate French with other subjects. The means to be employed are readings in French of material drawn from the fields of art, education, psychology, philosophy, social studies, natural sciences, literary criticism, etc., with reports in French where desired. Advanced phonetics, conversation, and letter writing are included.
Second year. 36 weeks, 6 credits.

French 3. History of French Literature. Miss Bradford.
The aim of the course is to become familiar with the masterpieces of French literature from the Middle Ages to the present day and to survey the works of minor importance; to develop the student's capacity to express, in correct French and with some degree of critical ability, his opinion of the works studied.
Third year. 27 weeks, 4½ credits.

French 4. Professionalized Subject Matter. Miss Bradford.
The aim of the course is to prepare teachers who possess professional knowledge and skills.
Systematic Grammar Review.
The aim is to acquire technical as well as functional knowledge of forms and syntax by means of thorough study of grammatical principles and rules together with passing of achievement tests.
Methodology: a. Theory.
The course presents in historical order the varied methods of acquiring and imparting the command of modern foreign language in accord with the fundamental principles of language psychology and of pedagogy. It includes a study of the nature of modern languages, methodology, objectives and measurement of instruction, purpose and content of courses, present-

day trends, texts, bibliography, realia, and other classroom materials, work-books, and other pupil aids, and preparation of the teacher.

The means to be employed are reading, reports, discussion, and, when possible, observation.

Methodology: b. Theory in Practice.

This is a course in demonstration of the most effective methods with preparation of unit and type lesson plans, making of exercises, drills and tests, preparing club or assembly programs, arranging bulletin boards, planning teaching devices, and assembling material.

Fourth year.   27 weeks, 4½ credits.

German 1.   Rudiments of Grammar and Elementary Readings.   (Elective).   Miss Bradford.
German for Beginners.

The broad aim of the course is to lead the pupil into a world of new experiences and thereby to develop in him a sense of pleasurable achievement or pride-power.

The particular aim is a progressive development of the ability to read, to write, to speak the foreign language and to understand it when spoken, with concurrent interrelation of all four skills. Attention is given to such knowledge of the grammar of the language as is demonstrated to be necessary for reading with comprehension and to lay a foundation for later acquisition of ability in all four skills. Emphasis is placed on careful reading of easy material and vocabulary. Use of realia and correlated reports in English on German civilization are a part of the building course.   First year.   36 weeks, 6 credits.

German 2.   Intermediate German.   (Elective).   Miss Bradford.

The aim of the course is the progressive development of the ability to read, to write, to speak German, and to understand it when spoken.

Continuous and abundant reading of well-graded texts is the chief means by which the aim is to be reached. Aural-oral exercises, grammar review, and written composition are added means. Classic short stories, a drama, poetry, a modern novel, and scientific selections are read. The history of German literature is surveyed.   Second year.   36 weeks, 6 credits.

MUSIC

Music 1.   Elementary Theory.   Miss Rand.

The aim of this course is to give the student a definite usable knowledge of music subject matter of moderate difficulty. All principles involved are to be used freely by the individual student in singing and in writing music.

The course includes a thorough study of the following: staff, using G, F, and C clefs; scales,—major, minor, and chromatic; intervals; note and rest values; key signatures for all major and minor keys; music terms of expression and tempo. The course also includes sight singing involving the progressive application of theory; and melody writing which involves the use of the eight measure period.

A study is made of the voice, and various exercises are given to promote free, beautiful tones. There is chorus practice of songs of standard worth. Each student is given practice in conducting.   First year.   18 weeks, 2 credits.

Music 2.   Music Appreciation.   (Elective).   Miss Rand.

The aim is to develop one's ability to listen to music with pleasure and intelligent discrimination in order to discover the following: mood, rhythm, melody, harmony, counterpoint, style, and elementary form. A study is made of the great composers from Bach to Stravinsky, with emphasis on the nationality of the composer, his place in music, and his best known compositions. A study is made of the instruments of the orchestra.

Throughout the course, suggestions are made for various types of lessons in music appreciation. Wherever possible, notes, pictures, and other materials helpful in teaching music appreciation, are collected and arranged.   Second year.   36 weeks, 4 credits.

Music 3. Teaching Music in the Elementary Schools. Miss Rand.

The aims of this course are as follows: (1) to inspire the student with the highest ideals of music teaching; (2) to classify and adapt to classroom use, the content of Music 1 (Freshman Theory); (3) to thoroughly familiarize the student with musical classroom procedure.

The course includes a study of the child voice through actual observation; a study of music methods for the first six grades by means of (1) examination of the best courses of study in selected school systems, and (2) demonstration lessons with children of the Training School.

Third year.   18 weeks, 2 credits.

Music Conference on Practice Teaching. Miss Rand.

During the time when the students are in the Training School, opportunity is given to teach music under direct supervision.   A general conference is held once a week for the discussion of problems common to all, for the demonstration of lessons which have been especially successful, and for constructive criticism.

The conference offers a very definite study of methods for the first six grades.   All students are present at all conferences.   Credits are included with those of Education 4.

Music 5. Elementary Harmony. (Elective). Miss Rand.

This course is for those students who wish a more thorough course in theory, and who may be interested in doing work in "Creative Music" in the grades. It consists of a thorough review of music theory; rhythmic and melodic dictation; melody writing; a study of the tonic, dominant, and subdominant triads, and the dominant seventh chord with their inversions. Some study is made of non-harmonic tones; and of simple modulation.

Third or fourth year.   27 weeks, 3 credits.

Music 6. Music History and Appreciation. (Elective). Miss Rand.

The aim of this course is to enrich the individual life of the student by a better understanding of great musical masterpieces and their historical backgrounds.   Periods of music from primitive to modern are studied.

Works such as the following are heard:

    1. Symphonies of Beethoven, Brahms, Tschiakowsky, and others.
    2. Scherherazade Suite . . . . Rimsky-Korsakow.
    3. Pictures at an Exhibition . . . . Moussorgsky.
    4. Les Preludes . . . . Liszt.
    5. Symphonic Poems of Strauss.

Toward the end of the course, some attention is given to junior high school music.

Third or fourth year.   27 weeks, 3 credits.

PHYSICAL EDUCATION
Health and Physical Education for Women

The purpose of the department of Health and Physical Education for Women is twofold:

1. Personal—to help each student to develop (a) in general physical efficiency; (b) in the knowledge of a variety of wholesome physical activities; (c) in the highest qualities of sportsmanship and leadership; and (d) in the best health understanding, attitudes, and habits.

2. Professional—to help the student to develop power in the leadership of children in health and physical education activities.

The total program includes (1) class work dealing with the subject matter, principles and methods in the fields of physical education and health, including examination of the courses of study and teaching materials used in the best elementary schools; (2) practice teaching in the student's own class and in the Training School; (3) the extra-curricular program conducted by the Women's Athletic Association, under the direction of student leaders, and including inter-group and inter-class contests and recreational and outing activities; (4) individual conferences and follow-up work with students needing advice as to the removal of defects or changes in habits of living; (5) guidance in individual corrective work for those having defects correctible by exercise.

Physical Education 1. Activities. Miss Caldwell.

This course offers analysis and practice of fundamental motor skills as they occur in an variety of activities; field ball, soccer, basketball, volley ball, quoitennis, tennis, dancing, and conditioning exercises. First year. 36 weeks, 2 credits.

Physical Education 2. Activities. Miss Decker.

This course is a continuation of Physical Education 1. It includes the game of field hockey in the fall term and during the remainder of the year gives emphasis to the fundamental physcial education activities for children with methods of teaching these activities at various age levels.
Second year. 36 weeks, 2 credits.

Physical Education 3a. Activities. Miss Caldwell and Miss Decker.

This course is a continuation of Physical Education 2. It includes more advanced activities suitable for adolescents and young adults. There is emphasis upon improvement in skills, bodily vigor, habits of cooperative play, powers of leadership; and capacities for enjoyment of activity. Within the limits set by facilities and time schedules there is offered some opportunity for the student to select activity in accordance with her particular needs and interests.
Third year. 27 weeks, 1½ credits.

Physical Education 3b. Theory of Physical Education. Miss Caldwell and Miss Decker.

This course offers a study of the fundamental principles underlying physical activity and its place in the process of education; a historical survey of this relationship in the various periods of human development; a study of the aims and objectives of the modern program in physical education in relation to contemporary educational purposes; an analysis of the values of the various types of activity such as games, sports, dancing, and stunts, in relation to the needs, interests, and ability of children of each sex and of different ages; a consideration of some of the practical problems in administering the program, with individual and group projects in planning and carrying out meets, playdays, pageants, festivals, and the like.
Third year. 27 weeks, 1½ credits.

Health Education 1. Personal and Community Health. Miss Caldwell.

A study is made of the fundamental habits of healthy living, with analysis of the simple biological and psychological factors underlying the health laws and of the personal and social implications of the health problem. First year. 36 weeks, 2 credits.

Health Education 2. School Health Education. Miss Decker.

This course deals with principles and practices in the health education of children; the physiological development of children in relation to school and community environment and individual health behavior; the function of the school in health guidance in cooperation with the home and with health education authorities outside the school.
Second year. 27 weeks, 1½ credits.

Physical Education for Men

The purpose of the department of Physical Education for Men is twofold:—

1. Personal—to provide an intelligent understanding of and practice in correct health habits; to develop ideals of sportsmanship, team-work, and leadership.

2. Professional—to train students adequately in methods of teaching games, sports, gymnastics, and in coaching. To develop skills in the individual sports, and in group games.

Physical Education 5. Mr. Meier.

Theory:—

This course consists of the study of personal hygiene, first aid, and the treatment of athletic injuries, including functions and care of the body with due stress on physiology and anatomy.

Activities:—

This course consists of general gymnasium work, including marching tactics, free-arm exercises, apparatus work, group contests and games. Instruction and practice are given in soccer, basketball, volley ball, baseball, track work, tennis, boxing, wrestling, tag football.

All men have the opportunity to take part in athletic contests under the intra-mural program.
First year. 36 weeks, 4 credits.

Physical Education 6.   Mr. Meier.

Theory:—

This course deals with the following problems: a study of methods of teaching health; the selection of schoolroom and playground activities for boys of different ages; methods of coaching and organizing groups.

Activities:—

General gymnasium work, practice and skills in the individual sports, and group games.

Second year.   36 weeks, 3½ credits.

Physical Education 7.   Mr. Meier.

Theory:—

This course consists of a study of the place of athletics in education, the history of athletics in American schools and colleges, and the planning of the high school athletic program, varsity, and intra-mural.

Activities:—

General gymnasium work, individual and group games and sports.   Practice coaching and the teaching of athletics.   Third year.   27 weeks, 3 credits.

Physical Education 8.   (Elective).   Mr. Meier.

This course offers special opportunities for developing varied skills in the individual sports and games.   Practice in coaching and officiating the major sports.

Seniors have opportunity to coach and officiate at intra-mural games in basketball, volleyball, baseball, boxing, and wrestling.   Fourth year.   27 weeks, ¾ credit.

SCIENCE

General Statement for Biology Courses.

Biology is a complex field and as such its satisfactory interpretation demands a varied method.

Class presentations are illustrated by living material, models, charts, lantern slides, opaque projection, still and motion films, and microprojection.

The laboratory experience includes use of wide-field binocular and compound microscopes, plant and animal experiments, studies and dissections of fresh and preserved specimens, maintenance of balanced aquaria and terraria.

Field excursions make real the class and laboratory studies.   Bridgewater affords an abundance of biological material.   Within easy reach from the campus are woods, fields, swamps, peat bogs, and ponds.   A nearby lake is a rich source of Protozoa, fresh water sponges, Planaria, Hydra, leeches, water insects, etc.   Poisonous plants, lichens, mosses, liverworts, club mosses, ferns, and wild flowering plants including the parasitic dodder and the insectivorous sundew and pitcher plant are studied in their native habitats.   Early morning bird trips are conducted for six to eight weeks each year during the spring migration period.

The Massachusetts State Course of Study in Elementary Science is used in the Training School.   Students during their training periods have an opportunity to participate in teaching various science units, a large percentage of which are biological.   Teaching suggestions and illustrative materials for these units are supplied by the biology instructor whenever possible.

Thus, by means of intrinsic subject matter and appropriate method, the courses in Biology are organized to make their contribution to the education of the teacher.

Science 1.   General Biology.   Miss Graves and Mr. Stearns.

This is a fundamental core course in which the beginning student is introduced to the basic principles of general biological science from a unified point of view.

The scope of biology and its relation to the other sciences are presented.

Both the plant and animal kingdoms are surveyed; then the more important phases of biology are presented in so far as the time allotment for the course permits.

First year.   18 weeks, 3 credits.

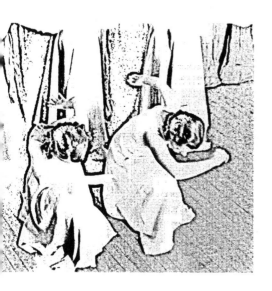

Science 2. Zoology. (Elective). Miss Graves.

A comprehensive view of animal biology is given by means of selected studies of the usual types representative of the great animal phyla considered in the order of their increasing complexity. Structure, functioning, adaptations, distribution, ecology, fossil records and economic importance are emphasized for the various forms.

The more familiar animal groups, i.e., fishes, amphibia, birds and mammals, receive considerable attention from the standpoint of their natural history.

Important biological relationships of natural balance, symbiosis, parasitism, communalism, commensalism, etc., find abundant illustration in the course.

Second year. 36 weeks, 6 credits.

Science 3. Botany. (Elective). Miss Graves.

This is a survey of the fundamental facts and principles of plant life. The structure and functioning of the higher plants are studied. The principal families of the flowering plants are reviewed and practice in identifying common species of both woody and herbaceous forms is given.

. Representatives of the great groups of the plant kingdom are found in the surrounding field and examined in the laboratory.

Topics such as methods of plant breeding, nature and control of plant diseases, plant communities and successions, climatic plant formations and the vegetation of the continents, economic plants and plant industries, furnish material for directed studies.

Third year. 27 weeks, 4½ credits.

Science 4. Advanced Biology. (Elective). Miss Graves.

Some of the major units that support the central thesis that all human progress is a biological phenomenon are as follows: a survey of the human body; human nutrition; bacteria, sanitation, and communicable disease; heredity and environment; genetics and eugenics; evolution; man from the farthest past; man's use of biological discoveries and inventions; scientific mindedness in adjusting to life. Fourth year. 27 weeks, 4½ credits.

Science 5. Gardening and Civic Biology. (Elective). Mr. Stearns.

The purpose of this course is threefold: (1) to furnish teachers with sufficient knowledge, skill, and experience so that they can take part in school and community gardening activities, (2) to give adequate knowledge for, and the real desire to cooperate in, the problems of nature study and science that arise in school and community life, (3) to introduce students to an activity that may prove to be of much personal and professional value and satisfaction throughout their lives.

The course deals with such matters as the following: (1) reforestation; flood prevention; fire prevention; bird protection; wild flower preservation and planting; insect extermination; eradication of such community pests as the rat, Gypsy moth, Dutch elm disease, white pine blister rust, Japanese beetle; (2) preparation of the soil; common garden plants, both flowers and vegetables, and how they are propagated; proper arrangement and cultivation of plots; planting and care of seed indoors and out; enemies, insect and fungus, with their remedies; fertilization of flowers; the potting and subsequent care of house plants; plants suitable for street and home grounds, and their planting; the making of lawns; tree and shrub planting; grafting and budding of apple and other trees. First year. 36 weeks, 2 credits.

Science 6. Elementary School Science for Teachers. Mr. Stearns.

This course furnishes the background of simple scientific knowledge necessary for teachers who are expected to follow the Massachusetts State Course in Science for Elementary Grades.

The course includes a study of the following:

WILD FLOWERS: habitat, identification, value, propagation, proper method of picking.

BIRDS: identification, migration, nesting habits, food, economic value; advice about making bird houses, bird-baths, bird traps.

TREES: a study of our common trees for identification purposes; study and comparison of the value of trees for street, home grounds, or forestry planting.

CULTIVATED FLOWERS: a working knowledge of the common cultivated flowers; various methods of propagation; preparation of the ground, care of plants; knowledge of pests and their control; planning of a vegetable or flower garden; methods of producing new kinds.

INSECTS: study of insects, including flies, mosquitoes, ants, bees, and others, and the controls.

SOIL: formation of soil; improvement; crops suited to certain soils; common rocks, minerals, and building stones.

NATURE TRAILS: help in laying out trails, of wild-flowers, trees, shrubs, and vines.

SKY: location of prominent heavenly bodies; planets, stars, and meteors; sun and moon.

ELECTRICITY: magnets; electric batteries; simple applications.

MISCELLANEOUS: water supply; thermometer; oxidation; fire-making, etc.

Second year. 18 weeks, 2 credits.

Science 9. Physical Science. (Required of and limited to those who take neither chemistry nor physics.) Mr. McGurren.

The purpose of Physical Science is to qualify the student to teach General Science up to the early years of high school. Students are afforded an opportunity for correlating the subject matter gained in this course with that of their prerequisite courses.

The course considers (1) the valid objectives of science; (2) the proper criteria of selection of subject matter; (3) a plan of organization of the subject matter for effective teaching; (4) a technique of classroom procedure which will insure the attainment of the objectives sought. The unit method is employed and the student submits lesson plans on each unit. The necessity of the inductive method of procedure is emphasized. Laboratory experiments and desk demonstrations accompany the subject matter lectures. Second year. 18 weeks, 2 credits.

Science 7. Chemistry. (Elective). Mr. McGurren.

A course in general college chemistry is offered to students desiring a scientific background for their curriculum.

The course consists of two one-hour lecture periods, and one two-hour laboratory period per week. A standard college textbook is used and the laboratory assignments correspond to the subject matter embodied in the textbook.

Each student is allotted an individual laboratory locker, fully equipped for the year's work. Each student is required to complete his full year's laboratory experiments in order to receive credit for the course. First year. 36 weeks, 6 credits.

Science 13. Applied Chemistry. (Elective). Mr. McGurren.

This course acquaints the student with problems in inorganic and organic chemistry that confront a teacher of general science.

Chemical phenomena of the home, the farm, and the factory are studied.

Two lecture periods a week deal with theory. The one hour of laboratory a week acquaints the student with the manipulation of apparatus, mixing solutions, desk demonstrations, and emphasis on dangerous chemicals and experiments.

First or second year. 18 weeks, 3 credits.

Science 14. Qualitative Analysis. (Elective). Mr. McGurren.

The standard method of group procedure is employed in the detection of the different cations and anions. The student is first acquainted with each metal in the five groups and then unknown solutions are given to be analyzed. All reagents are made by the students according to Normality, Molarity, and Percentage. Titration is also covered in this course.

Third year. 27 weeks, 4½ credits.

Science 8. Advanced Chemistry. (Elective). Mr. McGurren.

A course designed to prepare students anticipating teaching General Science and high school Chemistry. The subject matter is treated from a physical and mathematical aspect. Several different college texts are used to give the student practice in evaluating. The student is taught the practical aspects of laboratory management, such as buying, cataloguing, caring for equipment and stock, and laboratory technique. The course offers the student a good foundation in subject matter and the method of correlating laboratory experiments.

Fourth year. 27 weeks, 4½ credits.

Science 15. Physics. (Elective). Mr. Tyndall.
The study of heat, light, sound, electricity, and mechanics is developed in the light of present discoveries and the practical uses of them, as well as in past developments. Laboratory work is required.

The science teacher needs the complete subject matter and laboratory technique of this course, and so it is required for entrance into the senior seminar in science teaching.

Open to 1st and 2nd year students (either Physics A or a preparatory course in Physics is required for entrance.)   First year. 36 weeks, 6 credits.

Science 16. Physics A. (Elective). Mr. Tyndall.
A non-mathematical interpretation of physical phenomena as they relate themselves to our present life. Lectures, demonstration experiments, and occasional visits to industrial plants are used as the material for group discussions. The discussion groups not only help the student to understand better the place of physics in the world today, but also gives him a background that enables him to follow future developments in the field of science.

This course is intended for two classes of students: those who have no intention of following science in their teaching, but who feel a desire to have a general all-around background, and those who are not sufficiently grounded in the general aspects of the subject to take the major course in their first year. Physics A with Chemistry A satisfies the requirement of Physical Science in the second year.   First or Second year. 18 weeks, 3 credits.

Science 17. Advanced Physics. (Elective). Mr. Tyndall.
A discussion of the new developments in the field of science in their relation to physical theory. The relationship of energy and matter in radiation, electronic rays, transmutation, and similar topics are interpreted on the basis of present-day discoveries.

Open to Juniors and Seniors. (Physics 1 required.)
Third or fourth year. 27 weeks, 3 credits.

Science 18. Historical Geology. (Elective). Mr. Huffington.
This course offers a study of the evolution of the earth and its plants and animals. Such a study leads to a better understanding of the present earth features. Emphasis is placed on the geology of economic products.

Two term papers are required, one on a selected region, the other on the geology of a selected economic product.

This course is recommended to those specializing in geography.

Fourth year. 27 weeks, 3 credits.

SOCIAL SCIENCES

Social Science 1. Principles of Geography. Mr. Huffington and Mr. Tyndall.
This course aims to develop a knowledge of the principles of geography important in understanding how people are constantly making adjustments to their environment in an effort to solve their material needs, their occupational needs, and their higher needs. It also aims to develop a knowledge of the "geographic viewpoint" for use in the teaching of geography, together with enough knowledge of world environments to enable one to analyze geographic problems from any part of the world.

The content of this course is a study of the so-called "reciprocal relationships" existing between man and the following phases of his environment: land forms, water bodies, soils and minerals, location and climate, as worked out through a study of typical world situations illustrating these phases of the geographic environment.   First year. 18 weeks, 2 credits.

Social Science 2. Regional Geography West. Mr. Huffington and Mr. Tyndall.

This course aims to contribute toward an understanding of social, economic, and political problems from selected, western hemisphere regions. It also aims to present a "regional personality" of the respective regions through a scientific consideration of the resources within the area, their utilization by man, and possibilities for further utilization.

Representative natural regions studied are the following: (1) The New England-Canadian Maritime Region; (2) The Atlantic Coastal Plain; (3) The Gulf Coastal Plain; (4) The Corn Belt; (5) The Great Valley of California; (6) The Columbia Plateau; (7) The Amazon Valley; (8) The Peruvian Coastal Desert; (9) The Andian Highlands; (10) Mediterranean Chile; (11) The Brazilian Highlands; and (12) The Pampas. Second year. 18 weeks, 2 credits.

Social Science 3. Regional Geography East. (Elective). Mr. Huffington.

The viewpoint stated in Regional Geography (West) is also used in the study of the eastern hemisphere.

Representative natural regions studied are the following:

Europe: (1) Northwestern Highlands, (2) Northern Plains, (3) Interior Plains, (4) Southern Complex;

Asia: (1) The Delta Plains of China, (2) The Indo-Gangetic Plains;

Africa: (1) The Nile Valley, (2) The Sudan, (3) The Gold Coast, (4) South Africa.

Third year. 27 weeks, 4½ credits.

Social Science 4. Climatology. (Elective). Mr. Huffington.

This course develops, first, an understanding of the meteorological elements that are important in the make-up of weather; second, an understanding of world climatic types through an application of the principles of meteorology to a study of world climate and man's characteristics and dominant activities in selected world regions.

The content of this course consists of a study of pressure, winds, temperature, clouds, precipitation, cyclonic storms, anti-cyclones, special meteorological disturbances and a study of local weather. Also there is an analysis of the world distribution of the climatic elements. A term paper is required. Fourth year. 18 weeks, 3 credits.

Social Science 5. Anthropo-Geography. (Elective). Mr. Huffington.

This course aims to develop, first, some of the basic anthropo-geographic principles, and second, to give opportunity for application of these principles to a study of selected problems from American History.

The content of the first half of this course consists of an analysis of (1) the operation of geographic factors in history, (2) classes of geographic influences, (3) society and state in relation to land, (4) movements of people in their geographic significance, (5) the influence of selected geographic factors upon man's psychical make-up, and upon man's social and economic efforts.

The second half of this course includes a study of such problems as (1) the geographic influence of the Appalachian barrier upon colonial history, (2) the "westward movement" in relation to the physiographic features of the Appalachian system, (3) the geography of the Atlantic coast in its relation to the development of American sea power, (4) a study of immigration in relation to its geographic distribution, (5) sectionalism as influenced by geographic factors, etc.

A term paper is required which necessitates some research in the application of anthropo-geographic principles to a study of some current political or historical event.

Fourth year. 9 weeks, 1½ credits.

Social Science 6. Economic Geography. (Elective). Mr. Huffington.

This course presents a world survey of (1) the production of the principal basic commodities, (2) the distribution of the principal industries, and (3) the factors governing world trade. Emphasis is placed upon a study of current problems selected from the above phases of Economic Geography.

The content of the course consists of an analysis of the factors, especially critical environmental factors, affecting the production and distribution of (1) the world's chief agricultural products, (2) the world's products from mines, (3) the world's principal manufacturing industries and (4) the world's trade. Fourth year. 18 weeks, 3 credits.

Social Science 7. Survey of Civilization. Mr. Davoren.

The course begins with the observation of contemporary civilization to note its most obvious characteristics; search is made for the forces which constitute the driving powers in civilization, and for criteria for judging it.

The main features of the Industrial and Political Revolutions prior to the World War are traced. The significance of the War and the crises which followed are studied.

In dealing with recent events, emphasis is placed on standards of living, purchasing power, government regulation, the family, the school, recreational institutions, the state and the social aspects of disease, crime, urban life, nationalism, and international relations.

The course serves as an orientation to other social science courses as well as a preparation for more effective living. First year. 18 weeks, 3 credits.

Social Science 8. Ancient and Medieval History. (Elective). Miss Smith and Dr. Maxwell.

A history of western civilization from earliest times through the period of transition—the Renaissance and the Protestant Revolt—to modern times. Second year. 36 weeks, 6 credits.

Social Science 9. Modern European History. (Elective). Miss Smith.

A continuation of the study of western civilization beginning with the expansion of Europe and continuing to the present day. Some introduction to method as used in history teaching is given with an opportunity for some student-participation in trying out the various methods. Third year. 27 weeks, 4½ credits.

Social Science 10. American History for Elementary Teachers. Miss Smith.

This course covers the entire range of American history, stressing the important facts in their relation to the development of the American people. In addition, it offers training in good teaching procedures in history, and acquaintance with texts and workbooks in the elementary school field. Fourth year. 27 weeks, 4½ credits.

Social Science 11. American History. (Elective). Miss Smith.

This course is designed to give a complete review of American history to those students expecting to teach the subject. Beginning with the unit "Setting the Stage for Columbus," the study continues through the history of our country to the present day.

A teaching plan of the year's work such as would be suitable for use in junior or senior high schools is worked out by the students. The units are organized, and a study of the make-up of each is determined. An opportunity to give exploration, presentation, organization, and recitation lessons is afforded. Students plan and teach certain topics. Outlines, textbooks, workbooks, and bibliographies are evaluated. Fourth year. 27 weeks, 4½ credits.

Social Science 12. Principles of Sociology. Dr. Arnold.

The course is designed to give a better understanding of contemporary society, and to lay a foundation for dealing more successfully with social progress and the problems arising out of attempts to achieve it.

The nature of social data and the methods of studying them are dealt with briefly.

Types of personalities are analyzed. The process of building personality by the use of culture and social contacts is studied. Depth and breadth of personality are considered. The make-up, growth, and selection of population, and the origin of society are dealt with. A more extensive study is made of conflict, adaptability, cooperation, organization, equalization of opportunity, socialization, social control, liberation, commercialization, and professionalization. The process of reshaping society, the nature of social standards, and the problem of balancing the various social factors are included. Second year. 18 weeks, 2 credits.

Social Science 13. Advanced Sociology. (Elective). Dr. Arnold.

The theme of the course is social progress.

A brief survey is made of some theories of progress and the systems of several sociologists.

Lists of conditions favorable and unfavorable to progress are made. Exceptional individuals, ideals, public opinion, the environment, heredity and eugenics, political prerequisites, economic prerequisites, the family, internationalism, and morality are studied in relation to social progress.

The following problems are included: public health, immigration and internal migration, race, social aspects of physical and mental defectiveness, poverty, juvenile delinquency, criminology, industrial relations, social planning, and social reform. Students are urged to formulate an effective policy for dealing with each problem.

Much research is required as a foundation for understanding data and organizing them for teaching.   Fourth year. 27 weeks, 3 credits.

Social Science 14. Government in the United States. (Elective). Dr. Arnold.

The course aims to give a better grasp of the principles and problems of government. It prepares for teaching the political section of the Community Civics and Problems of Democracy courses.

The course deals with the development of the state and government, the function of modern government, and the division of function in the United States. It also includes a study of auxiliary controls, such as chambers of commerce and civic leagues, which play an important part in civic life.

The organization of local, state, and federal governments, and types of government activities—legislative, executive, and judicial—are studied.

The nature of political life and of citizenship are emphasized. The question of improving the quality of government receives much attention.   Third year.   9 weeks, 1½ credits.

Social Science 15. Principles of Economics. Dr. Arnold and Dr. Maxwell.

The course begins with the study of human wants, economic scarcity, and the struggle for economic opportunity, wealth, and power.

The factors of production—land, labor, capital, and business organization—are considered; also the return to these—rent, wages, interest, profits.

The greater part of the course deals with economic problems, including money, credit, banking, foreign exchange, the tariff, transportation, monopoly, trusts, the labor movement, social insurance, public finance, economic reform, and economic planning.

The course is designed to give insight into our present economic life and to prepare students to teach that part of the Community Civics course and Problems of Democracy course which lies in the field of economics.   Third year.   18 weeks, 2 credits.

REGISTER OF STUDENTS
1936–1937

Candidates for Three-Year Diploma
1937

Bromley, Marie Elizabeth..Bridgewater
Dix, Elizabeth Laila..Brockton
Jenkins, Isabel Aldana...Falmouth
Kirby, Dorthy Jean...Fall River
Moulson, Dorcas Elisabeth :...Ware
Santospirito, Angela Marie...Quincy

Candidates for Degree of Bachelor of Science in Education
1937

Agnetta, Frederic Nicholas...Dorchester
Allen, Elizabeth van de Sande..Wellesley
Alpert, Leo..Roxbury
Anderson, Anna...West Bridgewater
Bartell, Madeline Elizabeth..Norwood
Bartley, Mary Frances..Sandwich
Beaton, Nellie Grace..South Weymouth
Beck, Thelma Howard..New Bedford
Bell, Carolyn Chapin...Worcester
Bodwell, Verne Elwood...Bridgewater
Bonyman, Ella May..Quincy
Bowles, Edward Robert..Rockland
Bradford, Richard Edward...Kingston
Broderick, John Timothy (B. C.)...................................East Walpole
Brough, Frances Isabel...Fall River
Brown, Avis Arlene...Amesbury
Buckley, Margaret Mary...Brockton
Butterfield, Marjorie Irene..Lowell
Calen, Ruth Louise..South Weymouth
Callery, Margaret Anne...Bridgewater
Candy, Marjorie Ruth..South Weymouth
Cashin, Shirley Alice..Brockton
Cassels, Helen Margaret...North Attleborough
Cassidy, Marjorie Jackson..Plymouth
Chambers, Marion Charlotte...Wollaston
Chase, Milton Earle (Mass. State)................................Monument Beach
Cleary, Lillian May..East Braintree
Clifford, Joseph Nelson..Quincy
Cobb, Marjorie Bradford..Brockton
Cochrane, Virginia Treadwell...Wollaston
Colby, Phyllis...Merrimac
Collins, Louise Eudora...New Bedford
Conley, Elizabeth Catherine......................................East Taunton
Conley, Louise Agnes...Whitman
Connell, Emma Madeline...East Weymouth
Cosgrove, Edmund Gail..Lynn
Dacko, Helen Claire..Mattapan
Donahue, Katherine Marie...Somerset
Donahue, Mary Elizabeth..Taunton
Ehrhardt, Theodore Herman..Whitman
Eldridge, Louise...West Somerville
Farley, Rita Elizabeth...Pittsfield
Ferguson, Florence Mary..Rockland
Fiske, Edith Jessie..Greenfield
Foley, William James[1] (B. U.).....................................Randolph

Fuller, Marion Coombs..Wollaston
Gallipeau, Marion...Mansfield
Gillis, Florence Mabel..Brockton
Godsill, Catherine Mary..Brockton
Grant, Mary Eileen..Fall River
Gricius, Prakseda Lucy..Bridgewater
Hale, Elizabeth Farr (B. U.)...Athol
Hall, Dorothy Louise...Whitman
Hall, Eleanor Williams..Fall River
Hatchfield, Muriel Pauline..North Easton
Hayden, Christie Corinne..Brookville
Hinckley, James Francis...North Abington
Holmes, Daniel Luther..Newton
Horsman, Phyllis Alberta (Simmons)...................................Brockton
Horton, James Murray...Taunton
Houghton, Dorothea Ruth..Avon
Howland, Marjorie Ella...Elmwood
Imhof, Rosamond Leona...Abington
Jackson, Robert Copeland...Brockton
Jacobs, John William (Northeastern)......................................Quincy
James, Edith Virginia...Norwood
Jarusik, Helen...New Bedford
Julin, John Axel...Lexington
Kavanaugh, Catherine Lucille...Brockton
Kelleher, Virginia Rose..Winthrop
Kelly, Helen Marie...Holbrook
Kiernan, Vincent Owen..Randolph
Kimball, Beatrice May..Brockton
Kurtzman, Rose...Quincy
LaBelle, Quentin Victor..Avon
Lane, Agnes Helene...Natick
Lenzi, Leno Francis (Bates)..Plymouth
Leonard, George Melvin...Abington
Levow, Esther Anna..New Bedford
Lincoln, Doris...Wakefield
Long, Girard Joseph..Brockton
Lucey, Virginia Anne...Brockton
Lupica, Marion Rose..Brockton
MacDonnell, Jane Rita...North Weymouth
Macy, Bernigolde..Fall River
Madruga, Mary..New Bedford
Martini, Olga...Somerville
McDougall, Irving Alexander..Jamaica Plain
Medvetz, Charles Frederic..Abington
Metcalf, Ruth Elizabeth...Bridgewater
Moye, Ralph Ellis...Raynham
Nardozzi, Lena Mafalda..Stoughton
Nelson, Mary Elizabeth..West Bridgewater
Nelson, Ralph Henderson...Waltham
Newbury, Thomas William..Fall River
O'Sullivan, Nona Ruth..Randolph
Palmisano, Anna Marie..Quincy
Parsons, Gordon Fereday...New Bedford
Partridge, James Aloysius...Fall River
Pearson, Helen Dorothy..Middleborough
Pease, Reta Arlene..Amherst
Peebles, James Morris...Monument Beach
Penley, Frances Gould..Bridgewater
Perrier, Albert William Joseph (H. C.)..............................New Bedford
Pitcher, Damon Willard...Brockton
Place, Jessie May...Middleborough
Plaza, Jennie Anne...New Bedford

```
Puro, Alli Marion..........................................................Quincy
Quinn, Wilma Anna........................................................Holyoke
Randall, Marie.............................................................Whitman
Regan, William Alexander.............................................North Easton
Reidy, Mary............................................................East Weymouth
Rigby, Joan Eleanor..........................................................Quincy
Robak, Laura Helen.....................................................New Bedford
Roberts, Phyllis............................................................Arlington
Robertson, Helen MacGregor.............................................Norwood
Robinson, Harriet Elizabeth..............................................Littleton
Schapelle, Donald Thomas.................................................Rockland
Shaff, Anna Edith...........................................................Taunton
Shaw, Marion Ruth.........................................................Brockton
Sisson, Eleanor Marshall................................................New Bedford
Smith, Jeanette Woodbury..................................................Brockton
Spanick, Wanda Rosalie..................................................Pottersville
Stetson, Thomas Leslie................................................East Weymouth
Stewart, Ralph Boyd......................................................Weymouth
Studley, Lois Alyson (Clark Univ.)........................................Attleboro
Swartz, Philip..............................................................Roxbury
Thompson, Doris............................................................Bedford
Tindale, Helen Louise (Wheaton)...........................................Brockton
Tupper, Eleanor Winifred...................................................Abington
Tysver, Beulah Ione.......................................................Gloucester
vonBergen, Marie Hulda...................................................Wollaston
Westerling, Thelma Theresia.................................................Quincy
Westgate, Lawrence Bradford....................................................Rock
Weygand, Alma Louise.......................................................Taunton
White, George Sylvaria (B. C.)...........................................Mattapoisett
Whitney, Marjorie.......................................................West Yarmouth
Wilber, Philip Weston................................................Middleborough
Wilbur, Bernice Marie.....................................................Randolph
Zeolie, Richard Francis................................................East Weymouth
```
[1]Present part of first semester.

Candidates for Degree of Bachelor of Science in Education
1938

```
Barton, Beatrice Irene.....................................................Wollaston
Bazinet, Ernest Napoleon.....................................................Dudley
Bell, Dorothy Franklin.......................................................Brockton
Biller, Milton..............................................................Quincy
Blake, Eleanor Frances.....................................................Fall River
Blanchfield, Alice Joanne...............................................Easthampton
Borgatti, Magda Barbara.................................................Bridgewater
Bump, Benjamin James..................................................Middleborough
Cadwell, Emma Elizabeth.....................................................Kingston
Campbell, Eleanor Cavanaugh.............................................Bridgewater
Carlson, Margaret Laimi...............................................Middleborough
Carroll, Rita.............................................................Taunton
Chadwick, Alice Virginia.............................................West Bridgewater
Chassey, Viola Edith[2]...................................................Bridgewater
Chicetti, Joseph Anthony.................................................Bridgewater
Cleary, Marjorie Edith.....................................................Wollaston
Cleaves, Barbara Ruth................................................North Weymouth
Clegg, Elizabeth Anthony....................................................Seekonk
Cohen, Leo Henry............................................................Roxbury
Connell, Mary Alice....................................................East Weymouth
Costello, Margaret Ellen.....................................................Quincy
Courant, Genevieve Angelica...............................................Gloucester
Cowgill, Ethel May...........................................................Onset
```

Creney, Eileen Katherine..Brockton
Crowell, Geraldine Claire..Rockland
Cushman, Dorothy Roe..Bridgewater
Cushman, Milo Emerson, Jr..Westfield
Deane, Margaret Jessie..Bridgewater
Dennison, Doris Roberts..Quincy
Donahoe, Mary Rita..Weymouth
Donovan, Rita Frances..North Weymouth
Dutton, Shirley Mae..Plymouth
Dwyer, Richard Bernard..Huntington
Flaherty, Kathryn Edith..Lynn
Fleish, Sylvia..Acushnet
Foley, Grace Ellen..Randolph
Francis, Marilyn..Chelsea
Gallery, Mabel Jeanne..Fall River
Gardner, Claire Avis..Bridgewater
Gaudette, Wilder Ayling..Norwell
Gauszis, Mary Antoinette..Brockton
Goldstein, Mildred Roberta..Fall River
Graham, Kathleen Lyda....................................South Middleborough
Gurney, Elizabeth..New Bedford
Hanlon, Lawrence John..Quincy
Harlow, Eleanor Francis..Marshfield
Hartford, Marjorie Carroll..Gloucester
Hepperle, Anna Rosaline..Braintree
Hull, Pauline Torrey..Gloucester
Jagiello, Francis Gerard..Dorchester
Johnston, George Francis..Atlantic
Kelly, Kathleen Buddington..Springfield
King, Gertrude Lillian[1]..Haydenville
Kispert, Moira Estelle..Fall River
Knuttunen, Sylvia Vieno..Quincy
Koskela, Edward Werner..Sagamore
Kuchmeister, Florence Louise..Winthrop
Kundiz, Violet Jenny..Brockton
Leonard, Ardelle Meredith..Brockton
Lindsay, Josephine Mae......................................South Weymouth
Lipman, Dorothy..New Bedford
Logan, Helena Hope..South Weymouth
Martin, Jeannette..Plymouth
Masterson, Mary Ellen..Taunton
McCarthy, Daniel Justin..Brockton
McDonough, Mary Eileen..Norwood
McGloin, Margaret..Braintree
McGovern, John Francis......................................North Abington
Metcalf, Mary..Bridgewater
Moore, Marjorie Frances..Bridgewater
Morgan, Phyllis Evelyn..Springfield
Moynan, Dorothy..Taunton
Murphy, Rita Mae..North Weymouth
Nash, Malcolm Franklin..Abington
Newsome, Dorothea Wilma..Boston
Nolan, William Joseph..Dorchester
Nye, Alma Cassandra..Middleborough
O'Brien, Anna Irma..Quincy
Oram, Alice Louise..West Roxbury
Paul, Jeannette Aldora..Whitman
Perkins, Dorothy Rose..Plymouth
Perry, Amy Frances..New Bedford
Polsey, Barbara Steere..Attleboro
Powell, Margery Elizabeth..Middleborough
Radlo, Lucille..Roxbury

Rapaport, Jacob...Dorchester
Reynolds, Martha...Quincy
Riordan, Mary Rose...Brockton
Roberti, Ada Joan...Sandwich
Rudd, Marie...Boston
Russell, Marjory Floyd..East Bridgewater
Ryan, Albert Thomas..Rockland
Rymut, Bronia Bertha...Halifax
Sandlovitz, Helen Sylvia...Quincy
Shaw, Lillian Valencourt...New Bedford
Sherman, Dorothy Ellsworth...Eastondale
Sherman, June..State Farm
Skahill, Edward Vincent..Wellesley
Skerston, Olga Julia...Bridgewater
Smith, John Gregory...Dorchester
Smith, Margaret Emily...Buzzards Bay
Southworth, Elizabeth..Bridgewater
Sparkes, Alice Louise...Taunton
Spillane, Katharine Helen...East Braintree
Sullivan, Anna Elizabeth...Randolph
Sullivan, Lillian Marie..Quincy
Sullivan, Mary Elizabeth...Lowell
Sullivan, Ruth Mary..Fall River
Thomas, Gladys Trenetta...North Easton
Vanelli, Elaine Bona...Quincy
Vestburg, Dorothy Marie..Weymouth
Viner, Virginia Caroline..Quincy
Vollmer, Carol..Scituate
Warren, Thomas Larkin..State Farm
Waters, Doris Theothile..Roxbury
Webber, Helen Gertrude..Rutland
Wehter, Anne Kyllikki...Quincy
Weldon, Althea Virginia..Watertown
Whittemore, Dorothy Alice...Randolph
Wintermeyer, Charles...Weymouth
Witherell, Charles Emerson...South Worthington
Wynot, Rowena..Braintree
Zubrsycki, Victor..Bridgewater

[1]Present part of first semester.
[2]Present entire first semester.

Candidates for Degree of Bachelor of Science in Education

1939

Allan, Barbara Sawyer..Needham
Allen, Anne Dean...Fall River
Albertini, Albert Paul..Plymouth
Andrews, Louise..Quincy
Augustine, John...Bridgewater
Austin, Jane Elizabeth Montgomery.......................................Springfield
Bailey, Frank Merrill...Wareham
Barchi, Rita Edith..Seekonk
Bardini, Mary...East Wareham
Barnes, Marion Elizabeth..Taunton
Barrett, Mary Rita...South Braintree
Bartington, Betty Victoria[2]..Scituate
Barton, Amy Bertha..Attleboro
Behan, Geraldine Margaret..Holbrook
Bentley, Marjorie Frances...Weymouth
Bertoli, Lillian Theresa..Quincy
Black, Virginia Edith...Wollaston

Blaney, Robert Leonard ....Marion
Bongarzone, Elito....:..East Weymouth
Boyd, Gertrude Elizabeth...Quincy
Boyle, Dorothy Mary...Hatfield
Bragg, Meredith Gove..South Weymouth
Brine, Elizabeth Gertrude. -...West Newton
Burnett, John Raymond..Somerville
Butterfield, Esther Frances...Lowell
Campbell, Helen...East Braintree
Carlson, Judith Viola Maria..Springfield
Caspersen, Clara Carlottà...Holbrook
Chaput, Marjorie Louise...Haverhill
Cheetham, Dorothy Louise..Somerset
Chisholm, Mary Bernardette..Quincy
Church, Elsie Jane..South Braintree
Cole, Evelyn Arvilla..Attleboro
Connor, Gerald Joseph[2]..Watertown
Connors, Alice Elizabeth..Dedham
Coulter, Herbert Westley..Stoughton
Crooker, Frank Charles...Westborough
Cruz, Priscilla Elizabeth[1]...Onset
Currier, Gertrude Ricker...North Andover
Daley, Clement William..Brockton
Daly, Mary Agnes..Stoughton
Day, Harriet Olive..Norfolk
Denault, Edna Frances..Taunton
DeWolfe, Ellen Barbara...Quincy
DiNardo, Vincent James..Quincy
Dobson, Gladys Lorraine..Taunton
Dorosz, Alfred Frank..Bridgewater
Dunn, Harry Paul...Bridgewater
Dunphy, Mary Elizabeth...Randolph
Edwards, Helen Seale..Haverhill
Eisenhaure, Priscilla...North Reading
Emery, Rachel Adeline..Swansea
Farnham, Philip Clayton...Needham
Field, Dorothy Emily..Taunton
Fischer, Lilly Irene..Randolph
Fiske, Marjorie Gertrude...Greenfield
Francis, Lillian Mae...New Bedford
Fruzzetti, Adeline...Bridgewater
Galotti, Phyllis Federica...Braintree
Gannon, George Francis...East Weymouth
Gardella, Dora Rose Marie...Bradford
Gonet, Joanna Clara..Dartmouth
Groht, Elizabeth Adella..North Weymouth
Guzzi, Rosina..Wollaston
Haley, Alice Rita..Randolph
Hancock, Janet...Somerset
Hannigan, Walter Edward...South Boston
Harding, Walter Roy..Bridgewater
Hayden, Bettina Lillian..North Quincy
Heenan, Alice Mary...Rockland
Hegarty, Alice Rae[1]...West Wareham
Hern, Dorothy Helena..Taunton
Hill, Thelma Louise...Waltham
Hodgdon, William Bernard...South Weymouth
Holbrook, Barbara Thayer. -:....................................North Attleborough
Holtz, Clara Merium..Haverhill
Johnson, Victor Carl..North Easton
Judge, Mary Rose..Brockton
Kachan, Theresa...Northborough

Karimaki, Violet Lilly . . . . Quincy
Kaufman, Charles William . . . . Jamaica Plain
Kelleher, Rita Julia . . . . Brockton
Kelley, Helen Elizabeth . . . . Quincy
Keohan, Mary Gertrude . . . . Weymouth
Kiley, Dorothy Frances . . . . Milton
Lahey, Katharine Alice . . . . Plymouth
Lang, Rita Mary . . . . Holbrook
Lantz, Doris Elizabeth . . . . South Weymouth
Larsen, Carol Lillian . . . . North Dartmouth
Leonard, Rose Mary . . . . Weymouth
Lombard, Florence Harding . . . . Wellfleet
Lovett, Anna Elizabeth . . . . Hatfield
Luce, Walter Anderson . . . . Vineyard Haven
Lutted, Helen Hortense . . . . Stoughton
Lynch, Rosalie Marie . . . . Malden
MacLeod, Norma Louise . . . . Quincy
Madden, Margaret Regina . . . . Pittsfield
Matteson, Avis June . . . . Blackstone
Maurer, Ruth Lucille . . . . Cambridge
McFarlin, Thomas Huit . . . . Middleborough
McGhee, William Robertson . . . . Quincy
Metevier, John Louis . . . . Rockland
Moore, Mary Louise . . . . Bridgewater
Moriarty, Catherine Elizabeth . . . . Brockton
Morrissey, Margaret Theresa . . . . Rockland
Mosher, Ernine . . . . Somerset
Murphy, Joseph Francis . . . . Randolph
O'Hayre, Kathleen Elizabeth . . . . Rockland
Olsen, Verne Hamlyn . . . . Wrentham
Osgood, Carolyn Louise . . . . Wollaston
Osuch, Louise Nellie . . . . New Bedford
Paterson, Henry Finlayson . . . . Quincy
Payson, Margery Ward . . . . Brockton
Penley, Ruth Abbie . . . . Bridgewater
Perron, Laura Agnes . . . . Pittsfield
Perry, Robert . . . . Newtonville
Pickering, Priscilla Lottie . . . . East Blackstone
Pitkin, Alison Muriel . . . . North Andover
Procter, Clifford Russell . . . . West Somerville
Quigley, Mary Louise . . . . Milton
Reilly, John Clifton . . . . Bridgewater
Reinhalter, Marguerite Lillian . . . . Quincy
Reposa, Mary Elizabeth . . . . Seekonk
Rizzi, Helen Rose . . . . West Quincy
Roberts, Helen Rita . . . . Rockland
Roper, Sylvia Ann . . . . Princeton
Rosenthal, Leonard Ellis . . . . Dorchester
Ryce, Cynthia Alice . . . . Cambridge
Sanderson, Constance Taylor . . . . West Roxbury
Savaria, Eleanor Madeline . . . . Chicopee
Senesac, Edmond Everest . . . . New Bedford
Shaw, Charles Albert . . . . South Weymouth
Shaw, Madeline . . . . Middleborough
Shepherd, William Francis [3] . . . . Rockland
Sherman, Marion Frances . . . . Melrose
Shields, Mary Louise . . . . Rockland
Skoczulek, Joanna Marion . . . . New Bedford
Simon, Ruth Naomi . . . . Braintree
Smethurst, Clara . . . . Pottersville
Smith, Frances . . . . East Milton
Smith, Jean Elizabeth . . . . Westport

Snider, Helen Louise..Duxbury
Strange, Ruth Emma..Greenfield
Sweinimer, Christina...Brockton
Taylor, Henry Sidney..North Abington
Thebodo, Kathryn Mary.......................................Huntington
Thomas, Miriam...Wollaston
Torrey, Barbara Lois...Attleboro
Trulson, Beatrice Verna..Norwood
Turner, Dorothy Little...Saugus
Turner, Elizabeth Gray...Reading
Walmsley, Irma Violet[3].....................................New Bedford
Walton, Barbara..Saugus
Warren, Esther Georgette...Lee
Wastcoat, Elizabeth Jane...Wollaston

[1]Present part of first semester.
[2]Present entire first semester.
[3]Present part of second semester.

Candidates for Degree of Bachelor of Science in Education
1940

Allen, Mary Elizabeth..Taunton
Andrews, Mary Elizabeth..Brockton
Backman, Melvin Abraham...Lynn
Baltzer, Melba Elizabeth...Brockton
Batho, Jeanne Margaret...Hyde Park
Bissett, Ruth Margaret..Wollaston
Boutin, Lillian Eloise...Taunton
Bowley, Priscilla May...Randolph
Bradshaw, Florence Annie..Somerset
Breen, Annette Patricia...Belmont
Brennan, Mary Janice..Springfield
Briody, Mynette Margaret...Taunton
Brooks, Eleanor Craig...West Peabody
Buckley, Joan Ellen...North Weymouth
Buron, Rita Anne...Bridgewater
Callan, Francis Edward..Brockton
Cardoza, Ida..Taunton
Carter, Mercia...New Bedford
Chadwick, Ruth Esther.....................................West Bridgewater
Chambers, Virginia Ruth...Everett
Cole, Alice Hathaway..Plympton
Connelly, Winifred Mary..Medford
Crowley, Alice Marie.......................................North Weymouth
Curran, Claire Mary..Norwood
Daly, Phyllis Lee..Randolph
DeCoste, Mary Evelyn..Quincy
Deich, Samuel Isadore...Dorchester
Dobbyn, Barbara Elisabeth..Quincy
Dobbyn, Helen Josephine..New Bedford
Doherty, Genevieve Christine.....................................Cambridge
Drummey, Catherine Mary.......................................East Braintree
Dzenowagis, John..Bridgewater
Estey, Elsie Ruth...Canton
Fahey, Elizabeth Mary..Taunton
Farrell, Richard Joseph..Bridgewater
Fiore, Jordan Dominick..Fall River
Fisher, Olive Lucille...East Braintree
Fletcher, Hope Adams..Dudley
Foster, Elizabeth Ruth...East Sandwich
Freeman, Barbara Louise...Bridgewater

- 50 -

Gamble, Muriel Elizabeth . . . . Brockton
Garvey, Anne Frances . . . . Randolph
George, Ida Gertrude . . . . Wrentham
George, Irene . . . . Holbrook
Gerry, Zenon Andrew . . . . : . . . . Brockton
Gibson, Elizabeth Ann . . . . Gloucester
Greenwood, Helen Louise[1] . . . . Medford
Grundberg, Eleanor Marie . . . . Stoneham
Gysi, Erna . . . . Melrose
Hannan, Dorothea Christine . . . . : . . . . Brockton
Harris, George Foster . . . . Palmer
Harrington, Barbara Louise . . . . New Bedford
Harrington, Mary Bernardine . . . . Weymouth
Harrison, Eunice Claire . . . . Westport
Hatchfield, Rosalie Ann . . . . Whitman
Hathaway, Pauline . . . . Segregansett
Herrick, Elinor . . . . South Duxbury
Higgins, Agnes Elizabeth . . . . Whitman
Howes, Barbara Lee . . . . Stoughton
Jackson, Elsie Christina . . . . Arlington
Jenness, Ellwood Stephen, Jr. . . . . South Natick
Judge, Helen Frances . . . . Brockton
Kelly, Anna Ferriter . . . . Quincy
Kelley, Esther Louise . . . . Bridgewater
Kennedy, Thomas McEnroe . . . . Randolph
Killory, Martin Francis . . . . Brockton
Kimball, Elizabeth Janice . . . . East Walpole
Konrad, Stefani . . . . East Weymouth
Kotkov, Frederic . . . . Jamaica Plain
Kravif, Ruth Rebecca . . . . Fall River
Lamkin, Arnold Haskell . . . . Dorchester
Lang, Albert Anthony . . . . Holbrook
Lans, Rose Vellamo . . . . Walpole
Larson, Bertha Angelyn . . . . Attleboro
Latimer, Edgar Lloyd . . . . North Dighton
Laughlin, Winifred Marie . . . . Taunton
Lawler, Edith Margaret . . . . Nantasket Beach
Lesenechal, Elizabeth . . . . North Weymouth
Lesenechal, Joseph Jules, Jr. . . . . North Weymouth
Levenson, David Eli . . . . Brockton
Levine, Arnold . . . . Quincy
Lindquist, Rhea . . . . Avon
Lindsay, Jean Therese . . . . South Weymouth
Littlejohn, Lois Weston . . . . Middleborough
Lockary, Mary Gertrude . . . . South Weymouth
Logan, Muriel Elizabeth . . . . Wollaston
Lutted, Barbara Mildred . . . . Stoughton
MacFarland, Irving Phillips . . . . Bridgewater
Mador, Margaret Edith . . . . Cambridge
Manter, Loretta Whiton . . . . Taunton
Marquette, Nance . . . . Bradford
Martinelli, Alba . . . . Plymouth
Mattie, Irene May . . . . East Braintree
Mattson, Thelma . . . . Quincy
Mayo, Harriette Isabelle . . . . Orleans
McCann, Mary Agnes . . . . Chelsea
McCarthy, Margaret Mary . . . . Brockton
McDonald, Catherine Veronica . . . . West Quincy
McDonald, Cecilia Agnes . . . . East Weymouth
McGrory, Anna Louise . . . . Randolph
McHugh, Margaret . . . . East Walpole
McKean, Carrie Elizabeth . . . . Braintree

McLaughlin, Elizabeth . . . . Bridgewater
Meade, Margaret Mary . . . . Brockton
Meranda, Josephine . . . . Wareham
Merrey, Elizabeth May . . . . Bridgewater
Moore, Gladys Vernon . . . . Bridgewater
Mullin, Eleanor Mary . . . . Canton
Murphy, Margaret Eleanor . . . . Arlington
Mythen, Phyllis Marie . . . . Winthrop
Nerenberg, Arnold Lasrus . . . . Brockton
Newton, Betty . . . . Weymouth
Nickerson, Vernon Ward . . . . Orleans
O'Brien, Patrick Joseph . . . . Weymouth
O'Neil, Helen Virginia . . . . Attleboro
O'Rourke, Mary Juliette . . . . Quincy
Osberg, Constance Irene . . . . Fairhaven
Parent, Anna Elizabeth . . . . Stoughton
Pearson, Laura Barbara . . . . Middleborough
Pekarski, Virginia Anne . . . . Brockton
Peterson, Tyyne . . . . West Quincy
Pinand, Frances Eldora . . . . Monson
Pitts, Eleanor Anne . . . . Quincy
Prince, Barbara Elizabeth . . . . North Eastham
Purtell, Nan Frances . . . . North Adams
Queenan, Mary Irene . . . . Canton
Randall, Edwin Harold . . . . Natick
Raymond, Jane Lillian . . . . Buzzards Bay
Rice, Gordon Frederick . . . . Taunton
Richman, Sylvia Marilyn . . . . Brockton
Roderick, Mary Carman . . . . Somerville
Rodgers, William Herbert . . . . Taunton
Robinson, Dorothy Ellen . . . . Sturbridge
Russell, Dorothy Leith . . . . Attleboro
Sanford, Eileen . . . . Attleboro
Scanlon, Marie-Louise Delicia . . . . Middleborough
Shnitzler, Robert Karl . . . . Boston
Silveira, Winifred Mary . . . . Gloucester
Skulley, William Gerald . . . . Brockton
Smith, Elizabeth Bertha . . . . Dartmouth
Smith, Ruth McKenney . . . . Barre
Snow, Clara Marshall . . . . Quincy
Snow, Ruth Edna . . . . Mattapoisett
Spatz, Henry Maxwell . . . . Roxbury
Spencer, Marion Stone . . . . Weymouth
Staples, George Alvan . . . . North Dighton
Stein, Miriam . . . . Quincy
Studley, Marilyn Walker . . . . Rockland
Taylor, Barbara Weston . . . . Wellesley Hills
Taylor, Jean Wilson . . . . Westwood
Tebbetts, Helen Elizabeth . . . . Brockton
Tobin, Edward Bartholomew . . . . Rockland
Tobin, John Francis . . . . Bridgewater
Trenear, Lucille Doris . . . . South Weymouth
Tripp, Marion Agnes . . . . South Wareham
Trojano, Lena Anne . . . . Brockton
Tuomala, Norma . . . . Quincy
Tyndall, John Woodrow . . . . North Bellingham
Wall, Grace Margaret . . . . Brockton
Wall, Irma Aina . . . . Quincy
Wall, Margaret Mary . . . . Brockton
Walsh, Eleanor Elizabeth . . . . Quincy
Wardwell, Geraldine Frances . . . . Brockton
Wentworth, Alice Louise . . . . Braintree

Wheeler, Mildred Louise..New Bedford
Whiting, Jean Orr...Plymouth
Winsor, Elizabeth..Brockton
Woodbury, Doris Ellen...Abington
Woodward, Gertrude Kimball...................................East Norton
Woodward, Henry Francis...................................West Bridgewater
Wright, Elizabeth Stevens...Dedham
Wright, Marjorie Rita...East Braintree
Young, Barbara[1]...East Braintree
Zatuchny, Bernard Victor.......................................Dorchester
Zeolie, Harold Wilson.......................................East Weymouth
Ziemian, Phyllis Nancy......................................Indian Orchard
    [1]Present part of first semester.

Special Student

Sheehan, Dorothy Elizabeth..Worcester

SUMMARY

	Men	Women	Total
Candidates for Three -Year Diploma:			
1937..	...	6	6
Candidates for Degree of Bachelor of Science in Education:			
1937..	40	99	139
1938..	24	97	121
1939..	34	115	149
1940..	35	139	174
Special Student...............................	...	1	1
Totals for the year...........................	133	457	590
New admissions for the year 1936–1937...............	42	152	194
Graduated, 1936:			
Diploma...	...	12	12
Degree..	31	108	139
Whole number admitted from the beginning.............	1,883	9,193	11,076
Whole number of graduates:			
Diploma...	964	6,067	7,031
Degree..	231	730	961